PRAISE F

CREATIVE CONFIDENCE

"A five-star WOW! This wonderful, heartwarming book may literally change the world. Indeed, it must change the world. Don't just read it. *Use it.* Now."

—**TOM PETERS,** BESTSELLING AUTHOR OF *IN SEARCH OF EXCELLENCE*

"An indispensable field guide for creative explorers of all kinds. This compelling book will help build creative muscles for when you need them most."

—**TODD SPALETTO,** PRESIDENT, THE NORTH FACE

"Creativity is not magic, it's a skill. Get this book and learn the skill from the brothers who have taught it to more people—from nurses to bankers to teachers to computer scientists—than anyone else."

—**CHIP HEATH,** AUTHOR OF *MADE TO STICK, SWITCH,* AND *DECISIVE*

"A cross between Steve Jobs' commencement speech on creativity and a modern-day *What Color Is Your Parachute?,* the Kelley brothers offer simple but effective tools for the 'I'm not creative' set—business leaders and professionals seeking the confidence to innovate."

—**JOHN MAEDA,** PRESIDENT AND CEO, RHODE ISLAND SCHOOL OF DESIGN

"This is the only book about creativity that you'll ever need."

—**GUY KAWASAKI,** AUTHOR OF *APE: AUTHOR, PUBLISHER, ENTREPRENEUR*

"In hospitality—like in all industries—creativity is the life blood of engaging employees and guests (customers) and it is the capacity that allows you to strengthen your brand with every interaction. This book can help you engage powerfully with employees and customers and keep your brand relevant through changing times."

—**MARK HOPLAMAZIAN,** PRESIDENT AND CEO, HYATT HOTELS CORPORATION

"Tom and David have put together a practical, useful and generous book that's essential reading for anyone in the business of being creative."

—**SETH GODIN,** AUTHOR OF *THE ICARUS DECEPTION*

"I have long marveled at the Kelley brothers' ability to innovate in seemingly impenetrable fields (like health care). Now they've unfettered that power in all of us, sharing the tools and inspiring the confidence we need to find the very best solutions to complex problems we face at work—and in our personal lives."

—**GARY L. GOTTLIEB, M.D.,** PRESIDENT AND CEO, PARTNERS HEALTHCARE SYSTEM

"David and Tom have written an incredibly insightful book that challenges us all to have the courage to break out of our ruts, innovate, and create."

—**TIM KOOGLE,** FORMER PRESIDENT AND CEO, YAHOO

"Developing both the courage and confidence to create and the ability to cultivate original insight is of enormous practical importance, and this new book is the first place I send people to learn how it is done."

—**RICHARD MILLER,** PRESIDENT, OLIN COLLEGE

"David and Tom Kelley show us how to effortlessly dance between the creativity of elementary school and the pragmatism of the business world."

—**JOE GEBBIA,** COFOUNDER, AIRBNB

CREATIVE CONFIDENCE

ALSO FROM TOM KELLEY

The Art of Innovation:
Lessons in Creativity from IDEO, America's Leading
Design Firm

The Ten Faces of Innovation:
IDEO's Strategies for Defeating the Devil's Advocate and
Driving Creativity Throughout Your Organization

CREATIVE CONFIDENCE

UNLEASHING THE CREATIVE POTENTIAL WITHIN US ALL

TOM KELLEY
& DAVID KELLEY

WILLIAM
COLLINS

William Collins
An imprint of HarperCollins*Publishers*
77–85 Fulham Palace Road,
London W6 8JB
www.WilliamCollinsBooks.com

First published in Great Britain by William Collins in 2013

First published in the United States by Crown Business,
an imprint of the Crown Publishing Group, a division of Random
House LLC, a Penguin Random House Company, New York in 2013.

A catalogue record for this book
is available from the British Library.

ISBN 978-0-00-751797-8

Book design by Fabian Herrmann
Illustrations by Beau Bergeron, Alyana Cazalet, and Dan Roam
(see page 279 for a full list of credits)
Jacket design by Martin Kay
Author photo by Magnolia Photo Booth Co.

Typeset in Plantin

Printed and bound in Spain by Graficas Estella

MIX
Paper from
responsible sources
FSC
www.fsc.org   FSC® C007454

To Mom & Dad . . .
who gave us the freedom to express creative ideas,
and the confidence to act on them

CONTENTS

CREATIVE CONFIDENCE

PREFACE

This is a book from two brothers who have been close all their lives. As children in small-town Ohio, we played baseball on the same Tigers Little League teams in the summer and built snow forts together in the winter. We shared a bedroom for fourteen years, tacking up posters of muscle cars on the knotty-pine walls in the kind of finished basement that was popular in the Midwest. We went to the same grade school, joined the same Boy Scout troop, went on family vacations to Lake Erie, and once camped all the way to California and back with our parents and two sisters. We took many things apart, and put some of them back together.

But a close-knit relationship and overlapping lives do not mean our paths were the same. David has always been a bit unconventional. His favorite class in high school was art. He played in a local rock band called the Sabers with his friends. He built giant plywood structures like jukeboxes and grandfather clocks for the annual Spring Carnival at Carnegie Mellon. He started a firm called Intergalactic Destruction Company (the month *Star Wars* debuted in theaters) so he and his friends could do construction work together for the summer. Just for fun, he painted three bold green stripes along the back wall of our parents' house, still there forty years later. And he always loved creating one-of-a-kind gifts, like the time he made his girlfriend a phone that would dial only his number, no matter what buttons she pushed.

Tom, on the other hand, followed a path that seemed more traditional. After studying liberal arts in college, he considered going to law school, tried working at an accounting firm for a while, and played an IT-related role at General Electric. After getting an MBA, he worked in a spreadsheet-intensive position as a management consultant. Along the way, his jobs were mostly predictable, both in their day-to-day work and the longer-term career paths each offered. Then he joined the design world and discovered there was more fun to be had coloring outside the lines.

We remained close all this time and spoke to each other most weeks, even when we lived eight thousand miles apart. After David founded the design and innovation firm that would become IDEO, Tom helped out there during business school and then rejoined full-time in 1987. We have worked together ever since, as the firm has continued to grow: David as CEO and then chairman, Tom in leadership roles that included marketing, business development, and storytelling.

The story of this book begins in April of 2007, when David—the older brother—got a call from his doctor, who uttered one of the scariest, most dreaded words in the medical lexicon: *cancer*. He was at his daughter's fourth-grade class helping nine-year-olds think about how to redesign backpacks when the call came through, and he managed to spend another hour with the young students before breaking away to process this new setback. David had been diagnosed with squamous cell carcinoma—throat cancer—and given a 40 percent chance of surviving the ordeal.

At that moment, Tom had just wrapped up a presentation to two thousand executives in São Paulo, Brazil. As he sat down backstage and switched his cell phone back on, it rang almost immediately. When he got the sobering news of David's diagnosis, he abandoned the rest of his South American trip and headed straight for the airport. Although he knew there was little he could do to help, he had to get home to see David.

We had always been close, but David's illness further cemented our bond that year. Through the next six months of chemotherapy, radiation, hydration, morphine, and finally surgery, we saw each other almost every day, sometimes talking endlessly and other times passing hours together while speaking barely a word. At the Stanford Cancer Center, we crossed paths with patients who eventually lost their battle with cancer. We couldn't help wondering whether time was running out for David too.

If there is an upside to that terrible disease, it's that cancer forces deep reflection, causing you to think about purpose and meaning in your life. Everyone we know who has survived cancer says that they look at life differently in its aftermath. Late in the year, as David recovered from surgery, we saw the first real hope of pushing cancer into the background of our lives. Faced with that joyous possibility, we vowed that if David survived, we would do two things together that involved neither doctors nor hospitals: First, we'd take a fun brother/brother trip together somewhere in the world, which we had never done in our adult lives. And second, we would work together side by side on a project that would allow us to share ideas with each other and the world.

The trip was an unforgettable week in Tokyo and Kyoto, exploring the best of modern and ancient Japanese cultures. And the collaborative project was creating the book you now hold in your hands.

Why a book about creative confidence? Because we have noticed from thirty years at IDEO that innovation can be both fun and rewarding. But as you look at the sweep of your life and start to think of a legacy that survives beyond it, giving others the opportunity to live up to their creative capacity seems like a worthy purpose. In the midst of David's battle with cancer in 2007, a recurring question was "What was I put on Earth to do?" This book is part of the answer: To reach out to as many people as possible. To give future innovators the opportunity to follow their passions. To help individuals and organizations unleash their full potential—and build their own creative confidence.

David and Tom Kelley

THE HEART OF INNOVATION

When you hear the word "creativity," what do you think of next?

If you are like many people, your mind immediately leaps to artistic endeavors like sculpture, drawing, music, or dance.

You may equate "creative" with "artistic."

You may believe that architects and designers are paid to be creative thinkers, but CEOs, lawyers, and doctors are not.

Or you may feel that being creative is a fixed trait, like having brown eyes—either you're born with creative genes, or you're not.

As brothers who have worked together for thirty years at the forefront of innovation, we have come to see this set of misconceptions as "the creativity myth." It is a myth that far too many people share. This book is about the opposite of that myth. It is about what we call "creative confidence." And at its foundation is the belief that we are *all* creative.

The truth is, we all have far more creative potential waiting to be tapped.

We've helped thousands of companies bring breakthrough ideas to market—from Apple's first computer mouse to next-generation surgical tools for Medtronic to fresh brand strategies for The North Face in China. And we've also seen that our methods can produce a new creative mindset in people that can dramatically enhance their lives, whether they work in the fields of medicine, law, business, education, or science.

Over the past three decades, we've helped countless individuals nurture their creativity and put it to valuable use. They've created housing optimized for the needs of service men and women returning from war zones. They've set up an ad hoc innovation team in a corporate hallway, generating so much energy and noise that the company gave them a dedicated project space. They've developed a low-cost system for screening and fitting hearing aids among elderly villagers in developing countries, providing benefit to some of the 360 million people in the world who suffer from disabling hearing loss. The people we've helped have many backgrounds but share one common trait: they all have gained creative confidence.

Belief in your creative capacity lies at the heart of innovation.

At its core, creative confidence is about believing in your ability to create change in the world around you. It is the conviction that you can achieve what you set out to do. We think this self-assurance, this belief in your creative capacity, lies at the heart of innovation.

Creative confidence is like a muscle—it can be strengthened

and nurtured through effort and experience. Our goal is to help build that confidence in you.

Whether you think of yourself as "the creative type" or not, we believe reading this book will help you unlock and draw on more of the creative potential that is within us all.

CREATIVITY NOW

Creativity is much broader and more universal than what people typically consider the "artistic" fields. We think of creativity as using your imagination to create something new in the world. Creativity comes into play wherever you have the opportunity to generate new ideas, solutions, or approaches. And we believe everyone should have access to that resource.

For much of the twentieth century the so-called "creative types"—designers, art directors, copy writers—were relegated to the kids' table, far from serious discussions. Meanwhile, all the important business conversations took place among the "grown-ups" in boardrooms and meeting spaces down the hall.

But the creative endeavors that seemed fanciful or extracurricular a decade ago have now gone mainstream. Education thought leader Sir Ken Robinson—whose riveting 2006 TED Talk asking "Do Schools Kill Creativity?" was the most popular in history—says that creativity "is as important in education as literacy, and we should treat it with the same status."

In the business world, creativity manifests itself as innovation. Tech stars such as Google, Facebook, and Twitter have unleashed their employees' creativity to change the lives of billions of people. Today, in every department—from customer service to finance—people have opportunities to experiment with new solutions. Companies desperately need employees' insights from across the organization. No individual executive or division holds a monopoly on new ideas.

Whether you live in Silicon Valley or Shanghai, Munich or Mumbai, you've already felt the effects of seismic market shifts. Most businesses today realize that the key to growth, and even survival, is innovation. One recent IBM survey of more than 1,500 CEOs reports that creativity is the single most important leadership competency for enterprises facing the complexity of global commerce today. An Adobe Systems poll of five thousand people on three continents reports that 80 percent of people see unlocking creative potential as key to economic growth. Yet only 25 percent of these individuals feel that they're living up to their creative potential in their own lives and careers. That's a lot of wasted talent.

How might we shift that balance? How might we help the other 75 percent unleash their creative potential?

In 2005, David founded the d.school (formally known as the Hasso Plattner Institute of Design) to teach design thinking—a methodology for innovating routinely—to future entrepreneurs from Stanford's graduate schools. Originally, we thought that the primary challenge would be to teach creativity to people who saw themselves as "analytical types." We soon realized that all of the individuals we worked with *already* had creativity in spades.* Our job was simply to help them recapture it by sharing new skills and mindsets.

We have been stunned at how quickly people's imagination,

---

* A note about "we": This book has two authors, so you will see the first person plural a *lot*. When talking about just one of us, we will say "David" or "Tom." In some contexts, however, the "we" will mean the team at IDEO, where the two of us work, or the faculty and staff of the d.school, where David spends time.

curiosity, and courage are renewed with just a small amount of practice and encouragement.

For the people we've worked with, opening up the flow of creativity is like discovering that you've been driving a car with the emergency brake on—and suddenly experiencing what it feels like when you release the brake and can drive freely. We see this a lot with executives during workshops, or when we have clients in to collaborate side by side with us. They've sat through seminars about innovation before, and they are convinced they know how creative—or how *uncreative*—they're going to be. So when we get to a point that's fuzzy or unconventional—like doing an improv exercise—suddenly they whip out their smartphones, heading for the exits to make "really important" phone calls.

Why? Because they are insecure about their abilities in that setting. They instinctively fall back on the defense that "I'm just not the creative type."

In our experience, *everybody* is the creative type. We know that if we can get individuals to stick with the methodology a while, they will end up doing amazing things. They come up with breakthrough ideas or suggestions and work creatively with a team to develop something truly innovative. They surprise themselves with the realization that they are a lot more creative than they had thought. That early success shakes up how they see themselves and makes them eager to do more.

What we've found is that we don't have to generate creativity from scratch. We just need to help people rediscover what they already have: the capacity to imagine—or build upon—new-to-the-world ideas. But the real value of creativity doesn't emerge until you are brave enough to act on those ideas. That combination of thought and action defines creative confidence: the ability to come up with new ideas and the courage to try them out.

Geshe Thupten Jinpa, who has been the Dalai Lama's chief English translator for more than twenty years, shared an insight with us recently about the nature of creativity. Jinpa pointed out that there's no word in the Tibetan language for "creativity" or "being creative." The closest translation is "natural." In other words, if you want to be more creative, you just have to be more natural. We forget that back in kindergarten, we were all creative. We all played and experimented and tried out weird things without fear or shame. We didn't know enough not to. The fear of social rejection is something we learned as we got older. And that's why it's possible to regain our creative abilities so swiftly and powerfully, even decades later.

It turns out that creativity isn't some rare gift to be enjoyed by the lucky few—it's a natural part of human thinking and behavior. In too many of us it gets blocked. But it can be unblocked. And unblocking that creative spark can have far-reaching implications for yourself, your organization, and your community.

We believe that our creative energy is one of our most precious resources. It can help us to find innovative solutions to some of our most intractable problems.

CREATIVE CONFIDENCE IN ACTION

Creative confidence is a way of experiencing the world that generates new approaches and solutions. We know that *anyone* can gain creative confidence. We have witnessed it in people from diverse backgrounds and careers. Everyone—from scientists in their labs to senior managers at Fortune 500 companies—can approach life differently, with a new outlook and a larger tool set. Here are a few examples of people who have embraced creative confidence:

> Creative energy is one of our most precious resources.

- A former Olympian entered the airline industry and developed the confidence to tackle her company's crisis management problems head on. She gathered a volunteer task force of pilots, dispatchers, crew schedulers, and others to prototype procedures following weather-related flight disruptions, leading to a 40 percent faster recovery time.

- An army captain who served in Iraq and Afghanistan rallied over 1,700 people to petition for a pedestrian mall in the local community, proving you don't have to be a general to have an impact.

- Going beyond just the raw facts of a case, a law school student took a human-centered approach to her mock trial. She had the jury picture themselves at the scene of the incident to imagine what it felt like. And through harnessing their empathy, she won—the first time a jury had ever favored her side of that particular case.

- A former government executive started a grassroots innovation movement in Washington, D.C., that has grown to over a thousand members. Through workshops and networking events, she is spreading her new perspective on organizational change to other leaders and aspiring entrepreneurs.

- After four decades of experience, an elementary school teacher restructured her curriculum into design challenges. Instead of teaching discrete subjects, she created projects that covered the same topics but got students to step away from their desks and think more critically. Their test scores improved, but more important, parents noticed their children were more engaged and inquisitive.

You don't have to switch careers or move to Silicon Valley to change your mindset. You don't have to become a design consultant or quit your job. The world needs more creative policy makers, office managers, and real estate agents. Whatever your profession, when you approach it with creativity, you'll come up with new and better solutions and more successes. Creative confidence can inspire whatever work you already do—because you gain a new tool to enhance your problem-solving practices without having to abandon any of your existing techniques.

We've talked to doctors who have found new ways to empathize with and more effectively treat their patients, looking beyond the surface symptoms. We've talked to executive recruiters who use our methods to find new matchups between talented people and the companies that need them most. We've talked to social workers who use human-centered approaches to help people in the community understand confusing application forms.

People with creative confidence have a greater impact on the world around them—whether that means getting involved with their child's school, turning a storage room into a vibrant innovation space, or harnessing social media to recruit more bone marrow donors.

As legendary psychologist and Stanford professor Albert Bandura has shown, our belief systems affect our actions, goals, and perception. Individuals who come to believe that they can effect change are more likely to accomplish what they set out to do. Bandura calls that conviction "self-efficacy." People with self-efficacy set their sights higher, try harder, persevere longer, and show more resilience in the face of failure.

Our practical experience in the world of innovation and creative confidence aligns closely with his findings. When people transcend the fears that block their creativity, all sorts of new possibilities emerge. Instead of being paralyzed by the prospect of failure, they see every experience as an opportunity they can learn from. The need for control keeps some people stuck at the planning stage of a project. With creative confidence, they become comfortable with uncertainty and are able to leap into action. Instead of resigning themselves to the status quo, or what others have told them to do, they are freed to speak their mind and challenge existing ways of doing things. They act with greater courage, and have more persistence in tackling obstacles.

We believe this book will help you overcome the mental blocks that hold back your creativity. Chapter by chapter, we will give you tools that empower you to pursue new ideas with confidence. The stories, methods, and practices that we will share draw on decades of collaboration with creative thinkers everywhere, and we believe they will help you too.

THE CREATIVE CONFIDENCE QUEST

Today, our mission as authors is to help as many people as possible rediscover their creative potential.

Confronted with their newfound creativity, people sometimes confide in us that their mother was a dancer, or their father was an architect. They seem to be rationalizing their spark of creative energy, as if they are searching for concrete evidence. What they don't realize is that their creative potential was always a part of them—not because of any family history or genetic predisposition, but because it is a natural human ability within us all.

Creative confidence is a way of seeing that potential and your place in the world more clearly, unclouded by anxiety and doubt.

We hope you'll join us on our quest to embrace creative confidence in our lives. Together, we can all make the world a better place.

CHAPTER 1

$FLIP$

FROM DESIGN THINKING TO
CREATIVE CONFIDENCE

Doug Dietz is an earnest, soft-spoken Midwesterner with a wry, endearing smile and eyes that are quick to well up with tears at an emotional moment.

A twenty-four-year veteran of General Electric, Doug helps lead design and development of high-tech medical imaging systems for GE Healthcare, an $18 billion division of one of the largest companies in the world. His multimillion-dollar magnetic resonance imaging (MRI) systems peer painlessly inside the human body in ways that would have been considered magic just a generation ago.

A few years back, Doug wrapped up a project on an MRI machine that he had spent two and a half years working on. When he got the opportunity to see it installed in a hospital's scanning suite, he jumped at the chance. Standing next to his new machine,

Doug talked with the technician who was operating it that day. He told her that the MRI scanner had been submitted for an International Design Excellence Award—the "Oscars of design"—and asked her how she liked its new features. "It was a perfect example of bad interviewing technique," Doug says abashedly.

Doug was prepared to come away patting himself on the back for a job well done. But then the technician asked him to step out into the hall for a moment because a patient needed to get a scan. When he did, he saw a frail young girl walking toward him, tightly holding her parents' hands. The parents looked worried, and their young daughter was clearly scared, all in anticipation of what lay ahead—Doug's MRI machine. The girl started to sniffle, and Doug himself got choked up telling us her story. As the family passed by, Doug could hear their hushed conversation: "We've talked about this. You can be brave," urged the dad, the strain showing in his own voice.

As Doug watched, the little girl's tears rolled down her cheeks. To Doug's alarm, the technician picked up the phone to call for an anesthesiologist. And that was when Doug learned that hospitals routinely sedate pediatric patients for their scans because they are so scared that they can't lie still long enough. As many as 80 percent of pediatric patients have to be sedated. And if an anesthesiologist isn't available, the scan has to be postponed, causing families to go through their cycle of worry all over again.

When Doug witnessed the anxiety and fear his machine caused among the most vulnerable patients, the experience triggered a personal crisis for him that forever changed his perspective. Rather than an elegant, sleek piece of technology, worthy of accolades and admiration, he now saw that—through the eyes of a young child—the MRI looked more like a big scary machine you have to go inside. Pride in his design was replaced with feelings of failure for letting down the very patients he was trying to help. Doug could have quit his job, or simply resigned himself to the situation and moved on. But he didn't. He returned home and told his wife that he had to make a change.

So Doug sought advice on this deep personal and professional challenge from friends and colleagues. His boss at GE, who had encountered Stanford's d.school while at Procter & Gamble, suggested he try out an executive education class. Searching for a fresh perspective and a different approach to his work, Doug flew to California for a weeklong workshop. He didn't know quite what to expect, but he was eager to embrace any new methodology that would help him in his quest to make MRIs less frightening for young children.

The workshop offered Doug new tools that ignited his creative confidence: He learned about a human-centered approach to design and innovation. He observed and talked to users of existing products and services to better understand consumer needs. He collaborated with managers from other companies and industries on crude prototypes of designs to meet those needs. Gaining new perspectives from them, he continued to experiment and iterate his concepts in class, building on the ideas of others. At the end of the week, the cross-pollination of ideas made him feel more creative and more hopeful than he had when he left home. Going through the human-centered design process with people in diverse industries and roles—from management to human resources to finance—struck a chord in him. "I started to imagine how powerful this tool could be if I brought it back and got cross-functional teams to work together."

By applying human-centered design methods in his own work, Doug believed he could come up with a better solution for children—and he was determined to make it happen. He returned to Milwaukee knowing what he wanted to do. Without significant resources, funding, or support from his own company, Doug knew he couldn't launch a big R&D project to redesign an MRI machine from scratch. So he focused on redesigning the experience.

He started by observing and gaining empathy for young children at a day care center. He talked to child life specialists to understand what pediatric patients went through. He reached out for help from people around him, including a small volunteer team from GE, experts from a local children's museum, and doctors and staff from two hospitals. Next, he created the first prototype of what would become the "Adventure Series" scanner and was able to get it installed as a pilot program in the children's hospital at the University of Pittsburgh Medical Center.

By thinking holistically about how children experienced and interacted with the technology, Doug helped transform the MRI suite into a kid's adventure story, with the patient in a starring role. Making no changes to the complex technology inside the scanner, Doug and his ad hoc team applied colorful decals to the outside of the machine and to every surface in the room, covering the floor, ceilings, walls, and all of the equipment. They also created a script for machine operators so they could lead their young patients through the adventure.

One of the prototypes is a pirate ship worthy of an amusement park ride. The ship comes complete with a big wooden captain's wheel that surrounds the round opening of the chamber—a seafaring detail that also makes the small circumference seem less claustrophobic. The operator tells kids that they will be sailing

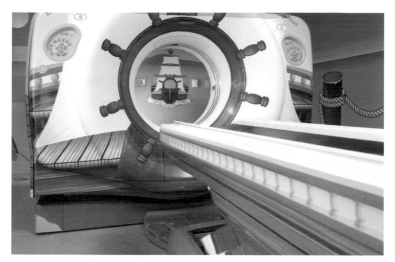
An MRI transformed into a pirate adventure for pediatric patients.

inside the pirate ship and they have to stay completely still while on the boat. After their "voyage," they get to pick a small treasure from the pirate's chest on the other side of the room. In another story, the MRI is a cylindrical spaceship transporting the patient into a space adventure. Just before the whirring and banging of the machine gets louder, the operator encourages young patients to listen closely for the moment that the craft "shifts into hyperdrive." This reframing transforms a normally terrifying "BOOM-BOOM-BOOM" sound into just another part of the adventure. Including the pirate experience and the rocket ship, there are now nine different "adventures."

With Doug's new MRI redesign for kids, the number of pediatric patients needing to be sedated was reduced dramatically. The hospital and GE were happy too because less need for anesthesiologists meant more patients could get scanned each day. Meanwhile, patient satisfaction scores went up 90 percent.

But the biggest satisfaction for Doug lies not in the numbers, nor in GE Healthcare's improved bottom line (although these were important for gaining internal support). His greatest reward came while talking with a mother whose six-year-old daughter had just been scanned in the MRI "pirate ship." The little girl came over and tugged on her mother's skirt. "Mommy," she asked, "can we come back tomorrow?" That simple question made all his effort worthwhile.

Less than a year after his epiphany, Doug's increased creative confidence catapulted him into a new role as a thought leader at GE. Would it be an exaggeration to say that, in the process, Doug also helped change the world a bit? Ask one of those young patients or their parents. They already have the answer.

A creative mindset can be a powerful force for looking beyond the status quo. People who use the creative techniques we outline are better able to apply their imagination to painting a picture of the future. They believe they have the ability to improve on existing ideas and positively impact the world around them, whether at work or in their personal lives. Without that belief, Doug wouldn't have been able to take the first step toward his goal. Creative confidence is an inherently optimistic way of looking at what's possible.

Doug's story illustrates the way human-centered design can lead to breakthrough innovations. New opportunities for innovation open up when you start the creative problem-solving process with empathy toward your target audience—whether it's kids or colleagues, clients or consumers. While competitors focused on the never-ending battle surrounding technical specifications (like scanning speed, resolution, etc.), Doug found a whole new way to improve the lives of patients and their families. In our experience, approaching challenges from a human perspective can yield some of the richest opportunities for change.

In every innovation program we have been involved with, there are always three factors to balance, represented by the three overlapping circles in the diagram below:

Finding the sweet spot of feasibility, viability, and desirability.

The first has to do with *technical factors,* or feasibility. In the early days of our work in Silicon Valley, this is where our clients always started. We've had clients present us with literally thousands of new technologies, from clever new wheel hubs for bicycles to new ways of chilling the human brain from the inside. A new technology—if it truly works—can be extremely valuable, and can provide the basis for a successful new company or a new line of business. Carbon fiber aircraft components, multi-touch interactive displays, and minimally invasive surgical tools all revolutionized their industries. But cool technology alone is not enough. If it were, we'd all be riding Segways and playing with robotic dogs.

The second key element is economic viability, or what we sometimes refer to as *business factors*. Not only does the technology need to work, but it also needs to be produced and distributed in an economically viable way. It needs to fit into a business model that will allow the enterprise to thrive. When we were growing up in the 1950s, *Popular Science* magazine suggested that twenty-first-century families would have their own personal helicopter in the backyard. So far, no one has come up with a clever business model to make helicopters affordable for ordinary people. The business factors on that concept just never lined up— and maybe never will. Even in nonprofit organizations, business factors can be critical. If you want to launch a program to increase the availability of safe drinking water in India or to build sanitation systems in Ghana, you need to find a way for it to pay for and sustain itself in the long run.

> Cool technology alone is not enough. If it were, we'd all be riding Segways and playing with robotic dogs.

The third element involves people, and is sometimes referred to as *human factors*. It's about deeply understanding human needs. Beyond just observing behaviors, this third aspect of successful innovation programs is about getting at people's motivations and core beliefs. Human factors aren't necessarily more important than the other two. But technical factors are well taught in science and engineering programs around the world, and companies everywhere focus energy on the business factors. So we believe that human factors may offer some of the best opportunities for innovation, which is why we always start there. And Doug did too, because GE's MRI machines already had great technology and business viability. Doug worked to understand how young children perceive MRI machines and what makes them feel safe when introduced to a new experience. Doug's empathy for his young patients led him to a breakthrough idea and ultimately assured his product's success.

Being human centered is at the core of our innovation process. Deep empathy for people makes our observations powerful sources of inspiration. We aim to understand why people do what they currently do, with the goal of understanding what they might do in the future. Our first-person experiences help us form personal connections with the people for whom we're innovating. We've washed other people's clothes by hand in their sinks, stayed as guests in housing projects, stood beside surgeons in operating rooms, and calmed agitated passengers in airport security lines—all to build empathy. An empathic approach fuels our process by ensuring we never forget we're designing for real people. And as a result, we uncover insights and opportunities for truly creative solutions. We've collaborated with thousands of clients to leverage the power of empathy, creating everything from easy-to-use lifesaving heart defibrillators to debit cards that help customers save for retirement.

We believe successful innovations rely on some element of human-centered design research while balancing the two other elements. Seeking that sweet spot of feasibility, viability, and desirability as you take into account the real needs and desires of your customers is part of what we at IDEO and the d.school call "design thinking." It's our process for creativity and innovation. There's no one-size-fits-all methodology for bringing new ideas to life, but many successful programs include a variation on four steps: inspiration, synthesis, ideation/experimentation, and imple-mentation. In our experience, an innovation or new idea may cycle through many iterations before the process is complete.

DESIGN-DRIVEN INNOVATION

Here's an overview of our approach to innovation, as de-scribed by IDEO partner Chris Flink. We adapt and evolve our methodologies continuously, so please feel free to make your own variations, as well, fashioning innovation techniques that fit your unique circumstances.

1. INSPIRATION

Don't wait for the proverbial apple to fall on your head. Go out in the world and proactively seek experiences that will spark creative thinking. Interact with experts, im-merse yourself in unfamiliar environments, and role-play customer scenarios. Inspiration is fueled by a deliberate, planned course of action.

To inspire human-centered innovation, empathy is our reliable, go-to resource. We find that connecting with the needs, desires, and motivations of real people helps to in-spire and provoke fresh ideas. Observing people's behavior in their natural context can help us better understand the factors at play and trigger new insights to fuel our innova-tion efforts. We shadow and do interviews with a variety of people out in the field. We speak to "extreme users," for ex-ample, discovering how early adopters make clever use of technology. Or, if we are redesigning a kitchen tool like a can opener, we may observe how elderly people use it to look for points of frustration or opportunities for improvement.

We look to other industries to see how relevant challenges are addressed. For instance, we may draw parallels between customer service at a restaurant and the patient experience at a hospital in order to improve patient satisfaction.

2. SYNTHESIS

After your time in the field, the next step is to begin the complex challenge of "sense-making." You need to recognize patterns, identify themes, and find meaning in all that you've seen, gathered, and observed. We move from concrete observations and individual stories to more abstract truths that span across groups of people. We often organize our observations on an "empathy map" (see Creativity Challenge #4, Chapter 7) or create a matrix to categorize types of solutions.

During synthesis, we strive to see where the fertile ground is. We translate what we've uncovered in our research into actionable frameworks and principles. We reframe the problem and choose where to focus our energy. For example, in retail environments, we've discovered that if you change the question from "how might we reduce customer waiting time?" to "how might we reduce *perceived* waiting time?" it opens up whole new avenues of possibility, like using a video display wall to provide an entertaining distraction.

3. IDEATION AND EXPERIMENTATION

Next, we set off on an exploration of new possibilities. We generate countless ideas and consider many divergent options. The most promising ones are advanced in iterative rounds of rapid prototypes—early, rough representations of ideas that are concrete enough for people to react to. The key is to be quick and dirty—exploring a range of ideas without becoming too invested in only one. These experiential learning loops help to develop existing concepts and spur new ones. Based on feedback from end users and other stakeholders, we adapt, iterate, and pivot our way to human-centered, compelling, workable solutions. Experimentation can include everything from crafting hundreds of physical models for delivering transdermal vaccines to using driving simulators for testing new vehicle systems to acting out the check-in experience at a hotel lobby.

4. IMPLEMENTATION

Before a new idea is rolled out, we refine the design and prepare a road map to the marketplace. Of course, rollouts can vary wildly depending on which elements of an experience or product are involved. Going live with a new online learning platform is very different from offering a new banking service. The implementation phase can have many rounds. More and more companies in every industry are beginning to launch new products, services, or businesses in order to learn. They live in beta, and quickly iterate through new in-market loops that further refine their offering. For example, some retailers launch pop-up stores as a way to test demand in new cities. And Boston-based startup Clover Food Lab began with a single food truck at MIT to gauge the market for its sustainable vegetarian food before the company committed to opening brick-and-mortar restaurant locations.

INNOVATING ROUTINELY WITH DESIGN THINKING

Design thinking is a way of finding human needs and creating new solutions using the tools and mindsets of design practitioners. When we use the term "design" alone, most people ask what we think about their curtains or where we bought our glasses. But a "design thinking" approach means more than just paying attention to aesthetics or developing physical products. Design thinking is a methodology. Using it, we can address a wide variety of personal, social, and business challenges in creative new ways.

Design thinking relies on the natural—and coachable—human ability to be intuitive, to recognize patterns, and to construct ideas that are emotionally meaningful as well as functional. We're not suggesting that anyone base a career or run an organization solely on feeling, intuition, and inspiration. But an over-reliance on the rational and the analytical can be just as risky. If you have a problem that you can't analyze easily, or that doesn't have a metric or enough data to draw upon, design thinking may be able to help you move forward using empathy and prototyping. When you need to achieve a breakthrough innovation or make a creative leap, this methodology can help you dive into the problem and find new insights.

IDEO uses this kind of thinking to help organizations in the public and private sectors innovate and grow. We help clients envision what their new or existing operations might look like in the future—and build road maps for getting there. Beyond the product development work Tom described in *The Art of Innovation,* we now have the opportunity to create new companies and brands, working with clients all over the world to help them launch new products, services, spaces, and interactive experiences. While we continue to work on products from toys to ATM machines, these days we are just as likely to create a digital toolkit to help consumers sign up for health care insurance or design a better education system for the country of Peru. In the last several years, we have worked directly with clients to help them embed innovation into the fabric of their enterprises.

Both at IDEO and in our client organizations, we've found that design thinking helps to foster creative cultures and build the internal systems required to sustain innovation and launch new ventures.

BORN TO FLIP—THE BIRTH OF THE D.SCHOOL

In the early 2000s, David started experimenting with team teaching at Stanford with professors from other parts of the university (like Terry Winograd from Computer Science, Bob Sutton from Management Science and Engineering, and Jim Patell from the business school). Prior to that, David had taught only students in the design division at the School of Engineering who already identified themselves as creative. In these new interdisciplinary courses, however, he worked with MBAs and computer science students who often didn't think of themselves that way.

It was in these classrooms that David and his colleagues could see what unlocking creativity really looked like.

Some of the students went beyond just using the tools and embraced the philosophy of design thinking, and in doing so, they developed a new mental outlook, a new self-image, and a new sense of empowerment. Students began visiting him during office hours—sometimes months after the class was over—to tell him that they had started to see themselves as creative individuals for the first time. That they could apply creativity to *any* challenge. Their eyes would light up with excitement, with a sense of opportunity, of possibility. Sometimes they cried.

David came up with a name for the transformation he was observing: "flipping"—changing from one state of mind to another. The playfulness of the term "flipping" reminded him of the joyful poetry of a somersault on a trampoline or a diving board.

These students he talked with were engaged and excited in a way that made it clear something in them had changed—permanently. It was the sort of profound impact educators live for.

Along with former student George Kembel (now executive director of the d.school), David began to talk with friends and colleagues about starting a new program. He envisioned a place in the university where students from different backgrounds could come to nurture their creative talents and apply their newfound skills to tough challenges. David pointed out that Stanford—like all world-class universities—had Nobel-laureate-quality researchers drilling deeper into their own fields of knowledge. But he suggested that there are tremendous challenges in the twenty-first century that aren't going to be solved that way. Maybe some solutions will be found by putting that scientist into a room with a businessperson, and a lawyer, and an engineer, and others. Rather than keeping all their eggs in the "going deep" basket, David proposed that Stanford make at least a small side bet on "going broad." And one day the new institute might have the respect and the cachet of the graduate school of business—commonly known as the "B-school." That's how the new venture got its nickname, which has stuck ever since: the "d.school."

When he told Hasso Plattner, one of the founders of enterprise software giant SAP, about the idea, Hasso generously reached for his checkbook. The d.school—officially known as the Hasso Plattner Institute of Design—opened its doors in 2005.

NURTURING CREATIVE THINKERS

While IDEO's work historically focused on innovations, from the beginning the Stanford d.school has focused on innovators. Students from every graduate school at Stanford come to take classes at the d.school. It doesn't issue degrees and doesn't have any required courses—everyone is there because they want to be. Currently more than seven hundred students attend courses at the d.school each year. Project-based classes are team taught by faculty members from all over the university and by industry practitioners. In this diverse environment, it's normal to hear many points of view—often conflicting ones. Students learn by doing and tackle real-world challenges, usually in multidisciplinary teams. Beyond just graduate students, executives from all over the world attend workshops, and the K-12 Lab works with children and educators (more than five hundred last year) to help spread confidence in their creative abilities.

Classes often start with simple design briefs—succinct articulations of a challenge—like "redesign the experience of getting your morning coffee." When confronted with a question or a problem such as the morning coffee challenge, people with strong

The d.school brings together ideas and people from all over the university.

analytical skills tend to snap instantly into problem-solving mode. They leap for the finish line and then start defending their answers.

For example, think about how quickly a skilled doctor—when presented with a set of symptoms   makes a diagnosis and prescribes a solution. Often it's a matter of seconds. During one morning coffee challenge a few years back, a med-school student in the class immediately raised a hand and said, "I know what we need: a new kind of coffee creamer." For such skilled analytical thinkers, an "unresolved" issue hanging in the air is uncomfortable. They are anxious to provide an answer and move on. In routine problem-solving situations, where there is a single right answer, that method is very efficient, and sometimes quite appropriate. Creative thinkers, however, confronted with the same open ended question, are careful not to rush to judgment. They recognize that there are many possible solutions and are willing to "go wide" first, identifying a number of possible approaches before converging on the ideas most worth implementing.

FLIP

So David and the d.school professors ask the students to set aside their initial answers—the cliché ones already in their heads. They encourage students to dig deeper, to understand the situation better, observing people's behaviors around coffee drinking in order to identify latent needs and opportunities. After the group has been guided through the design process in a collaborative environment, dozens of ideas emerge: everything from a coffeepot that knows exactly how hot you like your drink—and delivers it that way every time—to an automatic stirrer you drop into your cup. Then professors ask class members if any of the new solutions they arrived at were better than their initial ones. Usually, the answer is yes.

One prerequisite for achieving creative confidence is the belief that your innovation skills and capabilities are not set in stone.

A GROWTH STATE OF MIND

One prerequisite for achieving creative confidence is the belief that your innovation skills and capabilities are not set in stone. If you currently feel that you are not a creative person—if you think, "I'm not good at that kind of thing"—you have to let go of that belief before you can move on. You have to *believe* that learning and growth are possible. In other words, you need to start with what Stanford psychology professor Carol Dweck calls a "growth mindset."

Individuals with a growth mindset, Dweck says, "believe that a person's true potential is unknown (and unknowable); that it's impossible to foresee what can be accomplished with years of passion, toil, and training." She makes a compelling case, backed up by extensive research, that regardless of our initial talent, aptitude, or even IQ, we can expand our capabilities through effort and experience.

To fully appreciate the growth mindset, it helps to contrast it with its all-too-familiar evil twin, the fixed mindset. Consciously or unconsciously, people with a fixed mindset have the deep-seated belief that everyone is born with only a certain amount of intelligence and a certain amount of talent. If invited on a journey to creative confidence, people with a fixed mindset will prefer to stay behind in their comfort zone, afraid that the limits of their capabilities will be revealed to others.

Dweck explored the self-limiting nature of a fixed mindset in studying the behavior of freshman students at the University of Hong Kong. Since all classes and exams at the university are in English, incoming students who struggle with the English language are at a distinct disadvantage. After assessing the students' language skills and their mindset, Dweck asked the incoming students a question: "If the faculty offered a course for students who need to improve their English skills, would you take it?" Their answers revealed the power of mindset. "Students with the growth mindset said an emphatic yes. But those with the fixed mindset were not very interested." In other words, those under the influence of a fixed mindset were willing to sabotage their long-term chances for success rather than expose a potential weakness. If they let the same logic guide their choices throughout life, it's easy to understand how their perception of their own abilities as permanently limited can become a self-fulfilling hypothesis.

A growth mindset, on the other hand, is a passport to new adventures.

When you open your mind to the possibility that your capabilities are unlimited and unknown, you already have your running shoes on and are ready to race forward.

In reality, we all have a little of both mindsets. Sometimes the fixed mindset whispers in one ear: "We've never been good at anything creative, so why embarrass ourselves now?" And the growth mindset whispers in the other ear: "Effort is the path to mastery, so let's at least give this a try." The question is, which voice are you going to listen to?

MAKE YOUR DENT IN THE UNIVERSE

With creative confidence comes the desire to proactively guide the course of your life, or your organization, rather than be carried along on the prevailing winds. Roger Martin, dean of the University of Toronto's Rotman School of Management, once told us that what stuck out to him about designers is that they always act with intention. While others may unconsciously go with the default option, design thinkers make everything a conscious and original choice: from how they arrange their bookshelf to how they present their work. When they look around the world, they see opportunities to do things better and have a desire to change them. Once you start creating things, whether it's laying out a new garden or starting a new company or writing a new piece of code, you start to realize that everything has that intention behind it. Everything in modern society is the result of a collection of decisions made by someone. Why shouldn't that someone be you?

When you unleash your creative confidence, you start to see new ways to improve on the status quo—from how you throw a dinner party to how you run a meeting. And once you become aware of those opportunities, you have to start seizing them.

To us, that focused "intentionality" was one of Steve Jobs's defining characteristics. David met Steve back in 1980 when we designed the first Apple mouse. They became friends during a dozen subsequent projects for Steve's ventures at Apple, NeXT, and Pixar. Steve never took the path of least resistance. He never accepted the world "as is." He did everything with intentionality. No detail was too small to escape his attention. He also pushed us beyond what we thought we could do—we experienced his "reality distortion field" firsthand. He just kept raising the bar, even when it seemed unreasonable. But we would try, and we would get three-quarters of the way there, which was always farther than we would have gotten by ourselves.

Once you start creating things, you realize that everything has intention behind it.

After Steve was forced out of Apple and was planning the startup that would become NeXT Computer, he stopped by David's office one day to talk about his vision for the new machine. Always seeking Zen simplicity, Steve asked David, "What's the simplest three-dimensional shape in the world?" David was sure that it was a sphere. But that didn't matter, because the answer Steve was looking for was a cube. And so began our project of helping Steve with the engineering design of his cube-shaped NeXT computer.

During that intense project, Steve often called David at home in the middle of the night (in the era before e-mail and texting) to insist that we make some change. What kind of pressing issue couldn't wait until morning? One night, the call was about whether the plating on some screw on the inside of the cast magnesium cube should be cadmium or nickel. David's response was something like "Jeez, Steve, it's on the *inside* of the box." But Steve still cared—and we of course changed it. We don't know if any NeXT customer ever cracked open the machine and saw those perfectly plated fasteners, but Steve left no such details to chance.

Steve had a deep sense of creative confidence. He believed—he *knew*—that you can achieve audacious goals if you have the courage and perseverance to pursue them. He was famous for his exhortation to "make a dent in the universe," which he expressed this way in a 1994 interview:

> The minute that you understand that you can poke life and actually something will . . . pop out the other side, that you can change it, you can mold it, that's maybe the most important thing . . . Once you learn that, you'll never be the same again.

Steve's message was that we all have the ability to change the world. That was certainly true of Steve, a visionary who impacted so many people's lives and urged us all to "Think Different."

From Doug Dietz to Steve Jobs, all of the creatively confident people we've crossed paths with have found a way to apply extraordinary energy and exert remarkable influence. And we know that as you gain creative confidence going forward, you will have the chance to make your own dent in the universe. Start with a growth mindset, the deep-seated belief that your true potential is still unknown. That you are not limited to only what you have been able to do before. In subsequent chapters we'll offer practical tools that will help you to acquire new skills, find new inspiration, and unleash more of your creative capacities. To do so, you will need to act, and to experience your own creativity firsthand. But to act, most of us must first overcome the fears that have blocked our creativity in the past.

CHAPTER 2

$DARE$

FROM FEAR TO COURAGE

Picture a boa constrictor, draped casually around a man's neck. In the next room, a woman in a hockey mask and leather gloves stands warily behind a one-way mirror, watching them. Her heart is pounding. She has been terrified of snakes for as long as she can remember. Gardening and hiking have been out of the question, lest a garter snake slither across her path.

Yet here she is, about to walk into the next room and touch the snake of her nightmares.

How does she do it? How does she move from fear to courage?

The mastermind behind her phobia cure—leading the way for thousands more like her—is psychologist Albert Bandura. A Stanford researcher and professor, he has had a profound impact on the world of social learning and has been called the greatest living psychologist. Only Sigmund Freud, B. F. Skinner, and Jean Piaget ranked higher on a published list of eminent twentieth-century psychologists.

Bandura, now a professor emeritus at age eighty-seven, still works from his office at Stanford.

One day we got to talking about how to cure snake phobias. Basically it takes a lot of patience and small incremental steps, Bandura told us, but he and his colleagues could sometimes cure a phobia that has lasted a lifetime in less than a day.

First, Bandura tells phobic people that there is a snake in the room next door and that they are going in there—to which the typical response is "Like hell I am."

Next, he leads them through a long sequence of challenges, tailoring each subsequent step to be just within reach. For example, at one point, he has them look through a one-way mirror at a man holding the snake and asks, "What do you think this thing will do?" People with phobias are *convinced* the snake will wrap itself around the man's neck and choke him. But contrary to their beliefs, the snake just dangles lazily without choking or constricting at all.

And so it continues. Further along, Bandura asks them to stand at the open door of the room with the snake inside. If that step is too scary, he offers to stand with them at the door.

Many small steps later, eventually they are right there next to the snake. By the end of the session, people touch the snake. And just like that, their phobia is gone.

When Bandura began using this technique, he checked back with people months later and found that the phobia *stayed* gone, too. One woman even recounted a dream about a boa constrictor that helped her wash the dishes, instead of terrorizing her like the snakes in the nightmares she used to have.

Bandura calls the methodology he uses to cure phobias "guided mastery."

The process of guided mastery draws on the power of first-hand experience to remove false beliefs. It incorporates psychology tools like vicarious learning, social persuasion, and graduated tasks. Along the way, it helps people confront a major fear and dispel it one small, manageable step at a time.

This discovery—that guided mastery can cure a lifelong phobia in a short time—was a big deal. But Bandura discovered something even more meaningful during his follow-up interviews with the former phobics.

The interviews brought to light some surprising side effects. People mentioned other changes in their lives, changes seemingly unrelated to their phobias: they'd taken up horseback riding, they'd become fearless public speakers, they were exploring new possibilities in their jobs. The dramatic experience of overcoming a phobia that had plagued them for decades—a phobia they had expected to live with for the rest of their lives— had altered their belief system about their own ability to change. It had altered their belief in what they could accomplish. Ultimately, it transformed their lives.

This newfound courage, exhibited by the same people who once had to wear hockey masks to get near a snake, led Bandura to pivot toward a new line of research: how people come to believe that they can change a situation and accomplish what they set out to do in the world.

Since then, Bandura's research has shown that when people have this belief, they undertake tougher challenges, persevere longer, and are more resilient in the face of obstacles and failure. Bandura calls this belief "self-efficacy."

Bandura's work scientifically validates something we've been seeing for years: Doubts in one's creative ability can be cured by guiding people through a series of small successes. And the experience can have a powerful effect on the rest of their lives.

The state of mind Bandura calls self-efficacy is closely related to what we think of as creative confidence.

People who have creative confidence make better choices, set off more easily in new directions, and are better able to find solutions to seemingly intractable problems. They see new possibilities and collaborate with others to improve the situations around them. And they approach challenges with newfound courage.

But to gain this creative, empowered mindset, sometimes you have to touch the snake.

In our experience, one of the scariest snakes in the room is the fear of failure, which manifests itself in such ways as fear of being judged, fear of getting started, fear of the unknown. And while much has been said about fear of failure, it still is the single biggest obstacle people face to creative success.

THE FAILURE PARADOX

A widely held myth suggests that creative geniuses rarely fail. Yet according to Professor Dean Keith Simonton of the University of California, Davis, the opposite is actually true: creative geniuses, from artists like Mozart to scientists like Darwin, are quite prolific when it comes to failure—they just don't let that stop them. His research has found that creative people simply do more experiments. Their ultimate "strokes of genius" don't come about because they succeed more often than other people—they just do more, period. They take more shots at the goal. That is the surprising, compelling mathematics of innovation: if you want more success, you have to be prepared to shrug off more failure.

Take Thomas Edison, for example.

Edison, one of the most famous and prolific inventors in history, had failure baked into his creative process. He understood that an experiment ending in failure is not a failed experiment—as long as constructive learning is gained. He invented the incandescent lightbulb, but only after the lessons of a thousand unsuccessful attempts. Edison maintained that the "real measure of success is the number of experiments that can be crowded into twenty-four hours."

In fact, early failure can be crucial to success in innovation. Because the faster you find weaknesses during an innovation cycle, the faster you can improve what needs fixing. We grew up in Ohio, home of aviation pioneers Orville and Wilbur Wright. The Wright brothers are best remembered for what is sometimes called the "first flight," in December of 1903 at Kitty Hawk. But the focus on that accomplishment overlooks the hundreds of experiments and failed flight trials in the years that led up to that first successful flight. In fact, some reports suggest that the Wright brothers picked Kitty Hawk in part because the remote Outer Banks location would draw less media attention during their experiments.

The surprising, compelling mathematics of innovation: if you want more success, you have to be prepared to shrug off more failure.

Edison and the Wright brothers may seem like ancient history, but the tradition of learning from enlightened trial and error is still very much alive today. When Steelcase decided to reinvent the traditional classroom chair—eclipsing that uncomfortable wooden version with the writing surface rigidly attached to the chair arm—they worked with our design team to build over two hundred prototypes in all shapes and sizes. Early on, they experimented with small paper-and-Scotch-tape models. Later in the project, they constructed plywood components, attaching them to pieces of existing chairs. They went to local colleges, asking students and professors to interact with these "experience models" and give feedback. They carved shapes out of foam and fabricated parts on 3D printers to get a sense of shape and size. They prototyped mechanisms in steel. And as release to manufacturing approached, they built sophisticated full-size models that looked exactly like the real thing. All that relentless experimentation—and the associated learning—paid off. The Node chair replaced the rigidity of its predecessors with a comfortable swivel seat, an adjustable work surface, casters for maneuverability, and a tripod base to hold backpacks. The result is a mobile, flexible twenty-first-century classroom chair that quickly transitions from lecture-based seating to group activities, fitting with today's varied teaching styles. Launched in 2010, Node chairs are already in use at eight hundred schools and universities around the world.

Neither Edison nor the Wright brothers nor modern-day innovators like the design team on the Node chair were defensive or embarrassed about their method of trial and error. Ask seasoned innovators and they will likely have an impressive collection of "war stories" about failures on their path toward success.

DESIGNING FOR COURAGE

Albert Bandura used the process of guided mastery—a series of small successes—to help people gain courage and overcome deep-seated phobias. What would have been nearly impossible to accomplish in one giant leap became manageable in small steps, with the guidance of someone knowledgeable in the field. In a similar way, we use a step-by-step progression to help people discover and experience the tools and methodologies of design thinking, gradually increasing the level of challenge to help individuals transcend the fear of failure that blocks their best ideas. These small successes are intrinsically rewarding and help people to go on to the next level.

In our classes and workshops, we first ask people to work through quick design challenges, whether it's to redesign the gift-giving experience or to rethink their daily commute. We may jump in with some help or a small nudge, but mostly we let them figure out solutions themselves. Building confidence through experience encourages more creative action in the future, which further bolsters confidence. For this reason, we frequently ask students and team members to complete multiple quick design projects rather than one big project, to maximize the number of learning cycles.

At the d.school, one of the goals of getting people to work together on a project is to help them practice new skills and challenge themselves—and most likely experience failure as a result. We believe the lessons learned from failures may make us smarter even stronger. But that doesn't make failure any more *fun*. So most of us naturally try to avoid failure at all costs. Failure is hard, even painful. As Stanford professor Bob Sutton and IDEO partner Diego Rodriguez often say at the d.school, "Failure sucks, but instructs."

The inescapable link between failure and innovation is a lesson you can learn only through doing. We give students a chance to fail as soon as possible, in order to maximize the learning time that follows. Instead of long lectures followed by exercises, most of our classes at the d.school give students a little instruction up front and then get them working on a project or a challenge. We follow up in debriefs to reflect on what succeeded—and what can be learned from things that didn't work.

"Many d.school classes demand that student teams keep pushing the limits of possibility until they face-plant," says IDEO partner and consulting associate professor Chris Flink. "The personal resilience, courage, and humility born of a healthy failure form a priceless piece of their education and growth."

Facing failure in order to wipe away the fear is something understood intuitively by our friend John "Cass" Cassidy, lifelong innovator and creator of Klutz Press. In his book *Juggling for the Complete Klutz*, Cass didn't start us out juggling two balls, or even one. He began with something more basic: "The Drop." Step one is simply to throw all three balls in the air and let them drop. Then repeat. In learning to juggle, the angst comes from failure—from having the ball fall to the floor. So with step one, Cass aims to numb aspiring jugglers to that. Having the ball fall to the floor becomes more normal than the ball *not* falling to the floor. After we address our fear of failure, juggling becomes a lot easier. The two of us were skeptical at first, but with the help of his simple approach, we really did learn to juggle.

Fear of failure holds us back from learning all sorts of new skills, from taking on risks, and from tackling new challenges. Creative confidence asks that we overcome that fear. You know you are going to drop the ball, make mistakes, and go in a wrong direction or two. But you come to accept that it's part of learning. And in doing so, you are able to remain confident that you are moving forward despite the setbacks.

OVERCOMING FEAR OF CUSTOMER INTERVIEWS

We know from experience that our students often have a fear of venturing out onto the turf of customers and users in attempts to gain empathy with them. At the d.school, lecturer Caroline O'Connor and managing director Sarah Stein Greenberg have helped many students move past that fear, one step at a time. Here are a few ways of gaining empathy that they suggest, adapted for use in a business context. The techniques on the list start out easy and become increasingly challenging.

1. BE A "FLY ON THE WALL" IN AN ONLINE FORUM. Pay attention as potential customers share feedback, air their grievances, and ask questions. You're not looking for evaluations of features or cost; you're searching for pain points and latent needs among the people on the forum.

2. TRY YOUR OWN CUSTOMER SERVICE. Go through the experience of interacting with customer service, pretending to be a customer. Notice how your problem is handled, and how you feel along the way. Try mapping out the individual steps in the process and then graph the ups and downs of your mood or satisfaction.

3. TALK WITH UNEXPECTED EXPERTS. What does the receptionist have to say about your firm's customer experience? If you're in health care, talk to a medical assistant rather than a doctor. If you make a physical product, ask a repair person to tell you about what goes wrong with it.

4. PLAY DETECTIVE IN PURSUIT OF INSIGHT. Take some reading material and a pair of headphones to a retail space or an industry conference (or, if your customers are internal, an area where people tend to gather). Observe people's behavior, and try to figure out what is going on. How are they interacting with your product or service? What can you glean from their body language that indicates their level of engagement or interest?

5. INTERVIEW SOME CUSTOMERS. Think of a few open-ended questions about your product or service. Go to a place where your customers spend time, and find someone you are comfortable approaching. Tell them you'd like to ask a few questions. If the person refuses, no problem, just try someone else. Eventually you'll find someone who's willing—even dying—to talk to you. Press for more detail with every question. Ask "Why?" and "Can you tell me more about that?"—even if you think you already know the answer. Sometimes their responses will surprise you and point you toward new opportunities.

URGENT OPTIMISM

We can all learn something about effort and failure from the world of gaming. Author, futurist, and game designer Jane McGonigal talked to us recently about how video gaming can spark its own form of creative confidence. Jane makes a convincing case that harnessing the power of video games can have a major impact on life in the real world. In the realm of video games, the level of challenge and reward rises proportionately with a gamer's skills; moving forward always requires concentrated effort, but the next goal is never completely out of reach. This contributes to what Jane calls "urgent optimism": the desire to act immediately to tackle an obstacle, motivated by the belief that you have a reasonable hope of success. Gamers always believe that an "epic win" is possible—that it is worth trying, and trying *now*, over and over again. In the euphoria of an epic win, gamers are shocked to discover the extent of their capabilities. As you move from level to level, success can flip your mindset to a state of creative confidence. We've all seen this kind of persistence and gradual mastery of skills in children—from toddlers learning to walk to kids learning how to shoot a basketball.

Tom witnessed urgent optimism in action one Christmas morning when his teenage son Sean opened up a Tony Hawk skateboard video game and started trying it out. In addition to the usual on-screen action, the game comes with a controller that looks exactly like a real skateboard—minus the wheels. So there was Sean, balancing on a full-sized skateboard in the family room, surrounded by three generations of Kelleys. The family watched failure after failure as Sean's character on screen smashed into brick walls, skidded off of railings, and collided with other skaters. Potentially more embarrassing, Sean himself fell off the skateboard controller several times, nearly crashing through the glass coffee table beside him on the floor. But neither the on-screen calamities nor the occasional loss of balance in the physical world fazed Sean one bit. In the social context of the gaming world, he wasn't really failing—despite the noisy on-screen sound effects of his spectacular falls. Sean knew that he was on a path to learning. In fact, since reading about a video game is not much help, he was on essentially the *only* path available to gaining expertise.

By adapting the best attributes of gaming culture, we can shift people's view of failure and ratchet up their willingness and determination to persevere. We just need to hold out a "reasonable hope of success," as well as the possibility of a truly epic win. For example, in working with colleagues or on a team, we've found that if team members believe that every idea gets fair consideration, and that a meritocracy allows their proposals to be judged across divisional and hierarchical lines, they tend to put all of their energy and their creative talents to work on ideas and proposals for change. They work harder, persist longer, and maintain their urgent optimism when they believe victory is just around the corner.

But even after you overcome your initial fear of failure and gain creative confidence, you need to continue stretching yourself. Like a muscle, your creative abilities will grow and strengthen with practice. Continuing to exercise them will keep them in shape. All innovators need to make creative leaps: What need should you focus on? Which idea do you go with? What should you prototype? That is where experience and intuition come in.

Diego Rodriguez in his blog *Metacool* says that innovation thinkers often use "informed intuition" to identify a great insight, a key need, or a core feature. In other words, relentless practice creates a database of experience that you can draw upon to make more enlightened choices. When it comes to bringing new stuff into the world, Diego argues that the number of product cycles you've gone through (what he calls "mileage") trumps the number of years of experience. A twenty-year veteran of the auto industry who works several years on each new vehicle before it goes to market might have experienced far fewer cycles than a software developer working just two years on mobile apps that ship every couple of months. Once you have gone through enough rapid innovation cycles, you will gain familiarity with process and confidence in your ability to assess new ideas. And that confidence results in reduced anxiety in the face of ambiguity when you are bringing new ideas into the world.

PERMISSION TO FAIL

Whether you consider yourself a "born innovator" or are new to creative confidence, you can get better faster at coming up with new ideas if you give yourself and those around you the leeway to make mistakes from time to time. Permission to fail comes more easily in some settings than others. Venture capitalist Randy Komisar says that what distinguishes pockets of entrepreneurship like Silicon Valley is not their successes but the way they deal with failure. In cultures that encourage entrepreneurs, there is a greater appreciation and understanding of what Komisar calls "constructive failure."

Fear of risk and failure was a central theme when IDEO worked with German entrepreneur Lars Hinrichs on reinventing European venture capital. Research with software developers in the United States and Europe showed that the transition from a stable corporate job to the uncertainty of an early startup was one of the scariest moments in the evolution of a new venture. Many never managed to take that leap of faith. For lots of fledgling entrepreneurs, leaving the comfort and security of a salaried job stopped them in their tracks. So we structured the offering for Hinrichs's new early-stage investment company, HackFWD, to make that transition less intimidating. We helped give entrepreneurs a support network and resources so they could focus their efforts on what they do best. As part of HackFWD's "Geek Agreement"—published on the firm's website—entrepreneurs are paid roughly their current salary for a year as they push their concept toward the beta stage and one step closer to market and profitability. They also get connected to a network of experienced advisors. Quitting your day job remains a scary step, but maintaining your current income for a year makes it easier to pursue new-to-the-world ideas.

Within large companies, CEOs and executives have started to make similar efforts to reduce perceived risks and show their commitment to innovation initiatives. For example, VF Corporation— the world's largest apparel company and owner of dozens of familiar brands ranging from Nautica to The North Face—started an internal innovation fund a few years ago. Overseen by vice president of strategy and innovation Stephen Dull, the fund helps bootstrap innovative ideas at their earliest stages. It allows business unit managers to take entrepreneurial risks while meeting all the performance targets with their current product offerings. One successful innovation fund program explored whether VF's Wrangler brand, historically popular with cowboys in the American West, could be translated to appeal to motorcycle riders in India. The result was a line of jeans with features like water-repellent fabric that appeal to India's highly mobile youth market. To date, VF's innovation fund has sponsored more than ninety-seven such innovative ventures around the world.

We all need the latitude to try out new ideas. Look for ways to grant yourself creative license, or give yourself the equivalent of a get-out-of-jail-free card. Label your next new idea an experiment, and let everyone know that you are just testing it out. Lower others' expectations, so that failure can lead to learning without career damage.

EMBRACE YOUR FAILURES

An old proverb reminds us that "success has many fathers, but failure is an orphan." To learn from failure, however, you have to "own" it. You have to figure out what went wrong and what to do better next time. If you don't, you're liable to repeat your errors in the future.

Acknowledging mistakes is also important for moving on. In doing so, you not only sidestep the psychological pitfalls of cover-up, rationalization, and guilt; you may also find that you enhance your own brand through your honesty, candor, and humility.

Ask financial services professionals about their recent performance, and you are likely to hear a lot of "spin," as they either ignore their losses or cloud them with phrases like "market corrections" or "industry downdrafts." Nonetheless, one of our favorite examples of a company owning its failures comes from financial services. Bessemer Venture Partners is a well-respected, hundred-year-old venture capital firm that has gotten in on the ground floor of some stellar growth companies. Their website predictably features their "Top Exits." What's refreshing and not so predictable is that one click away from these mega-successes is a catalog of miscues and failed foresight Bessemer calls their "Anti-Portfolio." As Bessemer explains, their "long and storied history has afforded our firm an unparalleled number of opportunities to completely screw up." One of their partners passed over a chance to invest in the Series A round of PayPal, which sold a few years later for $1.5 billion. The firm also passed—seven times—on the chance to invest in FedEx, currently worth over $30 billion.

One of the firm's strongest advocates for the "Anti-Portfolio" idea, partner David Cowan, plays a starring role in its stories of missed opportunities and failures. A former neighbor of Tom's, Cowan lived within walking distance from the Silicon Valley garage where Larry Page and Sergey Brin started Google. Cowan was good friends with the woman who rented them the garage, and she tried to introduce him one day to these "two really smart Stanford students writing a search engine." Cowan's response: "How can I get out of this house without going anywhere near your garage?"

Bessemer's Anti-Portfolio is part of a trend among enlightened individuals and organizations who want to shine a bright light on their mistakes and learn from that dispassionate observation. The *Forbes* Midas List ranks Cowan among the top venture capitalists in the world for turning startup investments into gold. Could owning up to his failures have cleared the path for his outsized success?

Look around, and you will see other signs of this shift in thinking. Failure conferences are cropping up in Silicon Valley and elsewhere. Author and educator Tina Seelig asks her students to write a "failure résumé" that highlights their biggest defeats and screw-ups. She says that smart people accustomed to promoting their successes find it very challenging. In the process of compiling their failure résumé, however, they come to own their setbacks, both emotionally and intellectually.

"Viewing their experiences through the lens of failure forces them to come to terms with the mistakes they have made along the way," Tina writes in her book *What I Wish I Knew When I Was 20*. She is brave enough to include her own failure résumé, pointing out missteps such as not paying attention to company culture early in her career and avoiding conflicts in personal relationships. Now more aware and open about her early shortcomings, Tina is not held back by them. She's the executive director of the Stanford Technology Ventures Program, nurturing tomorrow's entrepreneurial leaders.

THE CLAY HORSE

Our fear of being judged is something we learn at a young age. But we don't start out with it. Most children are naturally daring. They explore new games, meet new people, try new things, and let their imaginations run wild.

In our family, that lack of fear manifested itself as a do-it-yourself attitude. If the washing machine broke, you didn't call a repair person. Instead you walked over to the washer, took it apart, and tried to fix it. That was part of the deal—in our house you were believed to be capable of fixing things.

Of course, sometimes home improvement jobs went awry. Once, we disassembled the family piano to see how it worked. Partway through the process, however, we realized that putting it back together wouldn't be nearly as much fun as taking it apart. What was once a musical instrument became more like a series of art objects. The giant harp-like array of strings from that piano is still leaning up against one wall of our former bedroom in the basement, and the beautiful assembly of eighty-eight wooden hammers is mounted today on a wall in David's studio.

Artistic license was tolerated as well. You could take a perfectly good red bicycle you'd gotten for your birthday, sandblast it the next day, and repaint it neon green, just to make it more interesting—without a word of recrimination.

We didn't know as children that we were creative. We just knew that it was okay for us to try experiments that sometimes succeeded and sometimes failed. That we could keep creating, keep tinkering, and trust that something interesting would result if we just stuck with it.

David's best friend in the third grade, Brian, had a different experience with creativity.

One day, David and Brian were in art class, sitting at a table with half a dozen classmates. Brian was working on a sculpture, making a horse out of the clay that the teacher kept under the sink. Suddenly one of the girls saw what he was making, leaned over, and said to him, "That's terrible. That doesn't look anything like a horse." Brian's shoulders sank. Dejected, he wadded up the clay horse and threw it back in the bin. David never saw Brian attempt a creative project again.

How often does something like that happen in childhood? Whenever we mention lost-confidence stories like Brian's to business audiences, someone always comes up to us afterward to share a similar experience when a teacher or parent or peer shut them down. Let's face it, kids can be cruel to one another. Sometimes, people remember a specific moment when they decided, as children, that they weren't creative. Rather than be judged, they simply withdrew. They stopped thinking of themselves as creative at all.

Author and researcher Brené Brown, who has interviewed scores of people about their experiences with shame, found that one third of them could recall a "creativity scar," a specific incident when they were told they weren't talented as artists, musicians, writers, singers.

When a child loses confidence in his or her creativity, the impact can be profound. People start to separate the world into those who are creative and those who are not. They come to see these categories as fixed, forgetting that they too once loved to draw and tell imaginative stories. Too often they opt out of being creative.

The tendency to label ourselves as "noncreative" comes from more than just our fear of being judged. As schools cut funding for the arts and high-stakes testing becomes more pervasive, creativity itself is devalued, compared to traditional core subjects like math and science. Those subjects emphasize ways of thinking and problem solving that have a clear-cut single right answer, while many real-world twenty-first-century challenges require more open-minded approaches. Well-meaning teachers and parents play a part when counseling young people toward conventional professions, sending the subtle message that occupations involving creativity are too risky and out of the mainstream. We both know what that feels like. Our guidance counselors told us when we were graduating from high school that we should stay near Akron, Ohio, and work for the local tire companies. They thought we were "dreamers" for setting our sights beyond the familiar. Had we taken their advice, there would be no IDEO or d.school today.

Education expert Sir Ken Robinson claims that traditional schooling destroys creativity. "We're now running national education systems where mistakes are the worst thing you can make," he says. "Education is the system that's supposed to develop our natural abilities and enable us to make our way in the world. Instead, it is stifling the individual talents and abilities of too many students and killing their motivation to learn."

Teachers, parents, business leaders, and role models of all kinds have the power either to support or suppress creative confidence in those around them. At the right age, a single cutting remark is sometimes enough to bring our creative pursuits to a standstill. Fortunately, many of us are resilient enough to try again.

Sir Ken told us a memorable story about talent that almost went to waste. He was born in Liverpool and made a discovery one day while talking to fellow Liverpudlian Paul McCartney. Apparently, the legendary singer-songwriter had not done especially well in his musical studies. His high school music teacher had neither given McCartney good marks nor identified any particular musical talent in him.

George Harrison had the same teacher and had likewise failed to attract any positive attention in music class. "Let me get this straight," Sir Ken asked McCartney in amazement, "this teacher had *half* of the Beatles in his classes and didn't notice anything out of the ordinary!?" Lacking encouragement from the person best positioned to nurture their musical talents, McCartney and Harrison could have "played it safe" and gone to work in Liverpool's traditional manufacturing and shipping industries. But that "safe" route would have put them in the center of a downward economic spiral. Liverpool's heavy industry declined precipitously in the following two decades, leading to dizzying unemployment in their hometown and eventually to the closing of the school they had attended, the Liverpool Institute High School for Boys. Luckily for music fans, McCartney and his friends John, George, and Ringo found encouragement elsewhere. And of course, the Beatles became one of the most successful and beloved groups of all time.

Much later, having achieved fame and fortune and been knighted by the queen, Sir Paul McCartney felt the noblesse oblige to help others get the creative chance he nearly missed. After the Liverpool Institute closed, putting his music teacher—and all the other faculty and staff—out of a job, McCartney helped restore the dilapidated nineteenth-century school building from the ground up. Together with educator Mark Featherstone-Witty, he formed the Liverpool Institute for Performing Arts, a thriving creative environment that helps young people with emerging talent build practical skills in music, acting, and dance.

LET GO OF COMPARISON

It takes courage to leave the land of certain outcomes and the comfort of what we know to try a new approach or share a wild-sounding idea. In her research on insecurity, Brené Brown talked with a thousand people to identify what makes them feel inadequate and to understand the downward spirals of feeling "not good enough." As Brown writes: "When our self-worth isn't on the line, we are far more willing to be courageous and risk sharing our raw talents and gifts." One way to embrace creativity, Brown says, is to let go of comparison. If you are concerned about conforming or about how you measure up to others' successes, you won't perform the risk taking and trailblazing inherent in creative endeavors.

Over the years, we've noticed from teams we've worked with that when people are insecure, they're not at their best. If they don't feel like they have the respect of their peers or their boss, they try to boost themselves through self-promotion. Instead of focusing on their work and feeling good about what they produce, they get sidetracked worrying about what other people think.

Once that insecurity takes hold, it can create a vicious circle. So whether you work alone or with a team, try hard to disarm it at the earliest opportunity. Give other people credit when it's due. Pay attention to signs that someone around you is feeling undervalued or has lost his or her self-confidence. Have that difficult conversation with the people around you to air out the issue. Because when you don't address insecurity, it's like the family secret that everyone knows but no one talks about. The conversation may be uncomfortable and painful but is often worthwhile in the long run.

We've seen the pattern dozens of times at IDEO where new employees are uncertain or tentative at first, trying to "be on their best behavior." And then over time, they let down their guard. You see the transformation in the way they dress and the way they act around people they see as authority figures. As they become more confident, they eventually adopt a bring-your-whole-self-to-work attitude and allow themselves to be vulnerable in a creative context. This vulnerability and ability to trust the people around you can help to overcome so many of the barriers to creative thinking and constructive behavior.

Our experience mirrors current research on resilience. Resilient people, in addition to being resourceful problem solvers, are more likely to seek help, have strong social support, and be better connected with colleagues, family, and friends. Resilience is often thought of as a solo effort—the lone hero who falls and rises up again to do battle. In reality, however, reaching out to others is usually a strategy for success. It doesn't have to be an admission of weakness. We need others to help us bounce back from adversity and hardship.

DRAWING CONFIDENCE

People who believe they lack creativity often insist, "I can't draw." More than any other skill, people see drawing as a litmus test for creativity. Everyone acknowledges that certain skills, like playing the piano, take years of training. But a common misperception is that we're either good at drawing, or we're not. In reality, drawing is a skill that you can learn and improve through practice with a little guidance.

A sketch is often worth a thousand words. Great communicators in today's fast-paced business world should never hesitate to reach for a marker pen. Unfortunately, most people shy away from the opportunity to sketch out their idea on the board. Or when they do, they preface their efforts with a disclaimer about their lack of drawing ability. Dan Roam, author of *The Back of the Napkin* and an expert on the art of visual thinking, says that roughly 25 percent of the businesspeople he works with are reluctant to even pick up a marker (he calls them "red pen" people). And another 50 percent ("yellow pen" people) are only comfortable highlighting or adding details to other people's drawings.

Dan helps people get over their hesitation to grasp the marker pen and approach the whiteboard by lowering the barrier. He does this by dissociating artistic drawing from drawing for communication. One of the lessons in his web-based "Napkin Academy" is called "How to Draw *Anything*." He insists that everything you ever need to draw on a whiteboard—or on a napkin—can be deconstructed into five basic shapes: a line, a square, a circle, a triangle, and an irregular shape he calls a blob. Next, he explains drawing fundamentals—such as size, position, and direction—that can seem comically simple yet still go underused. On the topic of size, for example, if you make one object bigger than another, your audience will understand that this object is either closer or—you guessed it—larger. And so it goes.

If you can draw the five shapes above (and we bet you *can*), then visual thinker Dan Roam says you are on your way to being able to draw anything—including people. With a focus on drawing for communication—not art—Dan can amp up your sketching skills in a matter of minutes. For example, Dan has three ways of drawing people (as he demonstrates for us below), depending on what you want to get across: 1. Stick figures are very simple and convey mood or emotion—especially if you make the head one third the total size of the person, so you have more room for showing expression; 2. Block figures add a rectangu-

lar torso and are good for showing motion or different body postures; 3. Blob figures (also known as "star" people) don't show emotion or action well but provide a quick way to draw groups and relationships.

ILLUSTRATION BY DAN ROAM.

When you sit with him in person over lunch, Dan draws non-stop on the tablecloth. It's hard not to come away from spending time with him a little bit more confident about your ability to communicate visually. Dan doesn't exactly teach you to draw. He just teaches you how to make better use of the simple drawing skills you already have.

Most of us accept that when we are learning a new sport like skiing, we will fall down, and other skiers on the slopes will see us with our faces planted in the snow. But when it comes to creative work, we tend to freeze up. And not just when we are novices. With people who draw well, perfectionism can be every bit as crippling as a lack of confidence in nondrawers.

We recently talked with two employees at IDEO from very different backgrounds. Yet both had the same fear of approaching the whiteboard in a business meeting. One was an industrial design intern with sophisticated drawing skills who had studied at the Art Center College of Design in Pasadena. The other was a business designer with a Harvard MBA and a bright analytical mind who didn't think of himself as artistic at all. The business guy didn't want to look silly trying to visually express an idea with a whiteboard sketch. And the skilled artist didn't want to be judged by the kind of drawing he could create in thirty seconds with a whiteboard marker in front of an impatient audience. One was hemmed in by timidity, the other by perfectionism. But the end result was the same. Each preferred to sit in his chair rather than risk being critiqued by his peers.

In other words, there are barriers on both ends of the skill distribution curve. As a result, good ideas go unexpressed, talent goes untapped, and solutions go undiscovered. We can all benefit from a nudge toward creative confidence. Non-artists need reassurance—and maybe a drawing lesson or two—so that they can express themselves in rough sketches when a picture is more powerful than words. And the artists need encouragement to set their perfectionism aside to draw a few simple lines that communicate the essence of their idea. Both need the kind of supportive culture that ignores the quality of their sketches and focuses on the quality of their ideas.

Wherever you fall on the artistic skill curve, half the battle is to resist judging yourself. If you can just grab a pen and stand up, you're halfway there. So take baby steps, as Bandura's phobics did. Walk up to a whiteboard in an empty room and draw an idea, just for practice. Then draw it again. We think you'll be surprised at how effective even a simple drawing of a concept can be—and how good it feels to get your idea across.

FROM FEAR TO JOY

Have you ever sat at a playground and watched a kid go down the slide for the very first time? That first time is scary for most children. There's a lot of initial reluctance even to climb the ladder. There's this frightened look on the child's face, a sense of "you want me to do *what*?" We know it's safe, but they don't. At first, they may need lots of support and encouragement just to get on the stairs. Some climb halfway up, get scared again, and climb back down. Finally, after watching other kids go down the slide crying "whee!" they make it all the way to the top and push off for the first time. And then the magic happens: their fear is replaced by exhilaration, by joy. Sometimes you can see their eyes widen as they realize how fast they're going. And just like that, they're on the ground again, with a huge smile on their face—and they want to run back to the ladder and do it all over again. The biggest hurdle is going down the slide that first time.

We see this same exhilaration on the faces of managers, scientists, salespeople, CEOs, and students after they've gone through their first design cycle and have emerged safely on the other side with a breakthrough idea. They are excited by their new ability, by the new tool in their toolbox. It's like riding a bike the first time without training wheels.

More than a century ago, poet and essayist Ralph Waldo Emerson urged us to "do the thing you fear, and the death of fear is certain." While the certainty Emerson offers may be arguable, the spirit of his advice remains just as powerful to this day. Looking back on your life, it's probably easy to think of "scary" things that became not-so-scary as soon as you tried them, whether it was jumping off the diving board, taking your first bite of a strange exotic food, or stepping up to the podium. And yet, in spite of all those successful, joyful experiences from the past, we cling to our fears whenever we encounter unfamiliar territory.

"Courage is only the accumulation of small steps."

Almost anyone can apply a "can-do" creative mindset to the challenges before them. And by layering design thinking methodology on top of your existing skills, you'll have more options to choose from in deciding on a course of action.

Throughout our lives, forces can push us toward or away from reaching our creative potential: a teacher's compliment, a parent's tolerance for tinkering, or an environment that welcomes new ideas. What matters most in the end, though, is this: your belief in your capacity to create positive change and the courage to take action. Creativity, far from requiring rare gifts and skills, depends on what you believe you can do with the talents and skills you already have. And you can develop and build on those skills, talents, and beliefs using methods described in the following chapters. After all, as Hungarian essayist György Konrád once said, "Courage is only the accumulation of small steps."

CHAPTER 3

$SPARK$

FROM BLANK PAGE TO INSIGHT

Sometimes a single course can change a student's life. That's what happened to Rahul Panicker, Jane Chen, Linus Liang, and later Naganand Murty when they used design thinking methods to move from blank page to insight to action. They turned a routine class assignment into a real-life product: the Embrace Infant Warmer, an easy-to-use medical device that costs 99 percent less than a traditional baby incubator and has the potential to save millions of newborns in developing countries.

The course was Design for Extreme Affordability, almost universally referred to at the d.school as simply "Extreme"— which pretty accurately describes both the pace and the class experience. Taught by Stanford business school professor Jim Patell and a faculty team, Extreme is a multidisciplinary melting pot in which students from departments all over the university come to the d.school to develop solutions for daunting, real-world problems.

Their project was to research and design a low-cost infant incubator for use in the developing world. No one on the team knew much about the complications of premature birth, let alone medical product design for other countries. They were electrical engineers, computer scientists, and MBA students—not public health experts.

Their first step was to look outward for inspiration. They decided to meet in an unconventional place on campus: high up in a tree, outside the CoHo coffee house. From that lofty perch, the four students Googled the global infant mortality problem and found statistics that astonished them. Each year, about fifteen million premature and low-birth-weight babies are born. A million of them perish, often within twenty-four hours of birth. The biggest preventable cause of death? Hypothermia. "These babies are so tiny they don't have enough fat to regulate their own body temperature," says Jane Chen, the MBA on the team. "In fact, room temperature feels like freezing cold water to them." In India, where nearly half of the world's low-birth-weight babies are born, hospital incubators can provide consistent, life-saving heat during those crucial first days. But traditional incubators can also cost as much as $20,000—each.

An obvious solution arose: the team could systematically reduce the cost of existing incubator designs by eliminating parts and using cheaper materials. Research done, right? And yet, one of the central principles of human-centered design is that you "empathize with the end user." Skipping that fundamental approach to innovation wasn't really an option. Instead, computer science team member Linus Liang got funding for a trip to Nepal in order to more deeply understand firsthand the unmet needs associated with incubators. What he saw there challenged his preconceived ideas and sparked creative insights that led to an innovative solution.

Linus was visiting a modern urban hospital in Nepal when he noticed something odd: Many of the hospital's donated incubators were empty. Puzzled, he asked why. Why were so many incubators empty if premature babies in the region needed them to survive? A doctor explained the sad, simple truth. Many of the hospital's incubators were going unused because the babies who needed them were often born in villages thirty miles away. No matter how inexpensive or well designed the incubator, life-and-death battles were being fought in the mother's home, not the hospital. And even if a new mother felt well enough to travel and had the family support she needed to maintain constant skin-to-skin contact with a premature baby en route to the hospital, she was still unlikely to leave her newborn in treatment. Family needs back in the village meant that premature babies were taken home again after five or six days, even if they should have stayed in an incubator for weeks.

Linus realized that incubator cost was just one design challenge in a complex web of human needs.

Back in Palo Alto, the team discussed what to do with these insights. On the one hand, there was a clear need for something that would help moms and babies in rural areas. On the other hand, as electrical engineer Rahul Panicker put it, "Dude, that's going to be hard." Should they stick with the technical challenge—designing a low-cost incubator for hospital use? Or tackle the human needs—designing a solution for mothers in remote areas? "We had mixed opinions on this," Rahul said. "Some people on the team wanted to do the more remote setting. . . . Others—and I was one of the others—wanted to do something that could actually get finished by the end of the class." Finally, they approached one of the teaching assistants in the class, Sarah Stein Greenberg (now managing director of the d.school), for advice. She told them, "You know, given a choice, I'd say, go after the hard challenge. That's what puts the 'extreme' in Extreme Affordability."

So instead of creating another hospital incubator, they reframed the design challenge as: *How might we create a baby-warming device that helps parents in remote villages give their dying infants a chance to survive?* For the Embrace team, the solution was now about the parent, not the clinician. They wrote this point of view down on the whiteboard in their workspace, and it became their guiding light for the rest of the twenty-week class—and beyond.

The team then worked to turn these insights into innovation. They did this by cycling rapidly through four or five rounds of rough prototyping to develop a simple but powerful solution. Shaped like a tiny sleeping bag, it contains a paraffin-based pouch that, once warmed in a heater, can maintain its temperature for up to four hours. The solution could be used outside of hospitals to keep a baby warm at the correct temperature anywhere in the world.

The Embrace Infant Warmer contains an inner heating pouch that keeps a baby warm for up to four hours.

Their next step: test the prototype with parents and stakeholders in rural villages.

They took the prototype to India, where they sought to understand the cultural nuances that could lead mothers to accept or reject the device. Along the way, they discovered factors they could never have found if they had stayed at home in Silicon Valley. For example, one day Rahul was in a small town in Maharashtra state showing the prototype to a group of moms. At that time, the prototype had a built-in temperature indicator, like the LCD thermometer on a fish tank or a fever strip that indicates a child's body temperature. When Rahul told the moms to warm the heating pouch to thirty-seven degrees Celsius to help regulate the baby's temperature, he got a surprising and unsettling response. One of the village mothers explained that in her community they believed Western medicines were really powerful, and often too strong. So if the doctor prescribed one teaspoon of medicine for her baby, she told Rahul, "I give him just half a teaspoon. Just to be safe. So if you ask me to heat it to thirty-seven, just to be safe I would heat it only to thirty or so." Alarm bells went off in Rahul's head.

Traditional engineers might have blamed this on random "user error" and moved on. But the Embrace team just iterated the design. Now, when the baby warmer reaches the correct temperature, an indicator simply changes to "OK," so there is no numeric value for parents to second-guess. In this instance, prototyping with end users in the field led to an improvement that may make the difference between life and death.

At the end of the class, the students faced a hard decision about what to do next. They could have stopped with a working prototype. Both Rahul and Linus had already started working at promising tech startups. Jane was fielding job opportunities as she finished her MBA. And one of the original team members, who had recently become a father, decided he couldn't continue to commit to the project full-time. In the end, however, the team couldn't let the project die. They began to apply to social entrepreneurship challenges and fellowships to raise the money to continue. Later they incorporated as a social venture and moved to India to launch their solution into the market. "At some level we did not have the heart to walk away," Rahul told us. "Knowing that we could have actually made a difference, but walking away because we had 'better opportunities'? No. I did not agree with that thinking. I wanted to devote the best years of my life to doing something meaningful."

For two years, the team traveled in India talking to moms, midwives, nurses, doctors, and shopkeepers. "The whole philosophy of Embrace is that you have to be close to your end user to make a really good design," says Jane. "Being here we have learned so much, and it's been critical to the success of this product." There were countless logistical hurdles to overcome. They had to keep iterating the design based on user feedback. "We were completely naïve," Rahul says. "We knew nothing about how to bring a medical device to market. How do you rigorously develop a product and test it and maintain standards while also maintaining low cost? How do people think about health care in towns and villages? How do goods and services reach there?"

In December of 2010, Embrace was featured in a segment of the ABC News show *20/20*. The show included images of a five-pound baby girl in Bangalore named Nisha, the first child to use the Embrace infant warmer in their clinical trial—and possibly the first life saved by the device. The show also included an emotional interview with a woman named Sudatha. She had lost all three of her newborn children, each a low-birth-weight baby too small to keep itself warm. Carefully examining the Embrace infant warmer, Sudatha observed, "If I had this . . . I could have saved my babies."

The team has come a long way since that TV episode aired: the company has now grown to ninety people. They continue to evolve the design of everything from the product itself to the distribution model to their organizational structure. They have begun selling the product to government facilities, giving them greater access to the poorest areas of India. But that institutional channel brought with it new constraints and required new design changes.

"Little did we know the time and capital it would require for us to get from a concept to a manufactured and clinically tested product—not to mention what it would take to build a distribution channel to sell our product," Jane wrote recently in a blog post for the *Harvard Business Review*. Another challenge they hadn't foreseen was that in spite of the compelling need for the product, they still had to persuade parents to change traditional behaviors to get them to use the new infant warmer. To increase acceptance, they have worked on educating mothers about hypothermia and conducted clinical studies to meet European medical device standards.

We don't know yet how many mothers will be spared Sudatha's fate, thanks to the team's inventiveness and perseverance. So far, however, they have helped over three thousand babies. And after launching a successful pilot program in India, they are working with NGO partners in nine more countries, have struck a global distribution deal with GE Healthcare, and recently have launched a version of the warmer that can be activated by hot water instead of electricity.

CULTIVATE A CREATIVE SPARK

Embrace began in Silicon Valley. But innovation—whether driven by an individual or a team—can happen anywhere. It's fueled by a restless intellectual curiosity, deep optimism, the ability to accept repeated failure as the price of ultimate success, a relentless work ethic, and a mindset that encourages not just ideas, but action.

The creative spark needed to come up with new solutions is something you have to cultivate, over and over again. One way to begin is to consciously increase the inspiration you encounter in your daily life.

Over the years, we've found several effective strategies to help you get from blank page to insight:

1. CHOOSE CREATIVITY: To be more creative, the first step is to decide you want to make it happen.

2. THINK LIKE A TRAVELER: Like a visitor to a foreign land, try turning fresh eyes on your surroundings, no matter how mundane or familiar. Don't wait around for a spark to magically appear. Expose yourself to new ideas and experiences.

3. ENGAGE RELAXED ATTENTION: Flashes of insight often come when your mind is relaxed and not focused on completing a specific task, allowing the mind to make new connections between seemingly unrelated ideas.

4. EMPATHIZE WITH YOUR END USER: You come up with more innovative ideas when you better understand the needs and context of the people you are creating solutions for.

5. DO OBSERVATIONS IN THE FIELD: If you observe others

with the skills of an anthropologist, you might discover new opportunities hidden in plain sight.

6. **ASK QUESTIONS, STARTING WITH "WHY?":** A series of "why?" questions can brush past surface details and get to the heart of the matter. For example, if you ask someone why they are still using a fading technology (think landline phones), the answers might have more to do with psychology than practicality.

7. **REFRAME CHALLENGES:** Sometimes, the first step toward a great solution is to reframe the question. Starting from a different point of view can help you get to the essence of a problem.

8. **BUILD A CREATIVE SUPPORT NETWORK:** Creativity can flow more easily and be more fun when you have others to collaborate with and bounce ideas off.

Let's look more closely at each of these, one by one.

CHOOSE CREATIVITY

Psychologist Robert Sternberg, who has done extensive research on intelligence, wisdom, creativity, and leadership for over thirty years, tells us that all of the creative people he has studied had one thing in common: at some point, they *decided* to be creative. They tend to:

- Redefine problems in new ways in order to seek out solutions.
- Take sensible risks and accept failure as part of the innovation process.

- Confront the obstacles that arise when challenging the status quo.
- Tolerate ambiguity when they are not certain that they are on the right path.
- Continue to grow intellectually rather than let their skills or knowledge stagnate.

"If psychologists wish to teach creativity," says Sternberg, "they likely will do better to encourage people to decide for creativity, to impress on them the joys of making this decision, and also to inoculate them for some of the challenges attendant on this decision. Deciding for creativity does not guarantee that creativity will emerge, but without the decision, it certainly will not."

Creativity seldom follows the path of least resistance. You need to deliberately choose creativity. One person who demonstrates how powerful that choice can be is Jill Levinsohn. Jill joined IDEO's business development team after working for six years in the advertising world, where "creatives" were a clearly designated group—an exclusive club to which Jill did not belong. "There were creative aspects of my job, for sure," Jill explains, "but there was a hard line between 'creatives' and people like me who supported them." One day at home, Jill chose to be more creative. She signed up for Pinterest, a social network for visually collecting and sharing online content like fashion ideas, recipes, and DIY projects. Before a friend's Cinco de Mayo party, she "pinned" a recipe for piñata cookies. Made of three layers with space in the middle one for a hidden cache of mini M&Ms, the colorful cookies captured people's imaginations. Within a week, her idea got repinned more than five hundred times. Jill kept at it, and to her surprise, people really liked her curation style. When her followers grew to over 100,000, she caught the attention of Pinterest itself. They featured her on the site, and by late 2012, Jill had attracted a *million* followers.

Jill says the experience has awakened her creative confidence. As an enabler of "creatives" in her advertising days, she used to see herself more on the sidelines of creativity. Now she sees sites like Pinterest as powerful tools for creative expression because the barrier to entry is "awesomely low," giving everyone the chance to exercise their creativity. "I'm taking more ownership of the fact that I'm doing something here, something to be proud of," says Jill. "Even if what I'm doing is not the most amazing or creative thing in the world, it can still be valuable."

Today, Jill sees her work with clients to be creative too. She recognizes that being creative doesn't have to mean starting from scratch or being the sole originator—it's about adding what you can, about making a creative contribution.

THINK LIKE A TRAVELER

Ever travel to a foreign city? We've all heard that "travel broadens the mind." But beneath this cliché lies a deep truth. Things stand out because they're different, so we notice every detail, from street signs to mailboxes to how you pay at a restaurant. We learn a lot when we travel not because we are any smarter on the road, but because we pay such close attention. On a trip, we become our own version of Sherlock Holmes, intensely observing the environment around us. We are continuously trying to figure out a world that is foreign and new.

Too often, we go through day-to-day life on cruise control, oblivious to huge swaths of our surroundings. To notice friction points—and therefore opportunities to do things better—it helps to see the world with fresh eyes.

When you meet creative people with lots of ideas constantly bubbling to the surface, you often come away feeling that they are operating on a different frequency. And they are, most of the time. They have all their receptors on—and frequently turned up to eleven. But the fact is, we are all capable of operating in this mode.

Try to engage a "beginner's mind." For kids, everything is novel, so they ask lots of questions and look at the world wide-eyed, soaking it all in. Everywhere they turn, they tend to think, "Isn't that interesting?" rather than "I already know about that."

At the d.school, to demonstrate the power of rediscovering the familiar, we often take executives to places like a gas station or the airport. They assume they know exactly what an airport is like. So we have them sit down and watch how the passengers are lining up, how they get their bags off the carousel, how they talk to the airline representatives. Most leave the airport feeling surprised at what they noticed for the first time. Like the passengers sitting alone at a gate who had arrived for their flight four hours early "just in case." Or the busy mom who is paying all her bills as boarding begins. Or the "safety rituals" people perform, like tapping the side of the plane three times as they step on board.

Rediscovering the familiar is a powerful example of how looking at something closely can affect what you see. So apply a beginner's mind to something you do or see every day: commuting to work, eating dinner, or preparing for a meeting. Look for new insights about familiar things. Think of it as a treasure hunt.

By adopting the eyes of a traveler and a beginner's mindset, you will notice a lot of details that you normally might have overlooked. You put aside assumptions and are fully immersed in the world around you. In this receptive mode, you're ready to start actively searching out inspiration. And when it comes to inspiration, quantity matters. For example, part of what makes venture capitalists so business savvy—and ultimately so successful—is that they see a lot more ideas than ordinary people. Young, enthusiastic entrepreneurs come to them every day with new-to-the-world business ideas in search of funding. In the VC business, it's called "deal flow." All other things being equal, the better your deal flow, the more successful your venture capital firm will be.

What's true of deal flow for venture capital firms is true of *idea* flow, too: the more fresh new ideas cross your field of vision each day, the greater your insights will be. As Nobel laureate Linus Pauling famously said, "If you want a good idea, start with a lot of ideas." At IDEO, we try to keep a fast-running stream of conversations going about provocative new technologies, inspiring case studies, and emerging trends.

MAKE A COMMUNITY CHALKBOARD

One way to find inspiration is to ask questions in an unexpected space, either online or in physical locations. In our San Francisco office, we have a floor-to-ceiling chalkboard in one of the restrooms. It serves as an informal forum and gives us a quick read of what's going on and what's on people's minds. Questions like "What fun things can we do this year?" or "What healthy snacks would you recommend to a friend?" adorn the board. Sometimes an unfinished draw-ing—an empty aquarium, for example—may inspire visual additions.

To create your own community chalkboard, here are a few tips from IDEO senior experience manager Alan Ratliff:

EXPERIMENT FIRST. Try out different sizes and placements before you commit to changing the walls. We started with a small chalkboard and then scaled it up after the idea took off. We now apply black chalkboard paint directly to the walls for maximum flexibility.

CHOOSE A MEDIUM. Although we use whiteboards in most of our meeting rooms, chalk on a chalkboard is a fun al-ternative. It is inviting and easily erasable, so people don't think twice about adding to or changing what's there.

PROMPT FOR IDEAS. Blank slates are intimidating. So get things rolling with a leading question or a drawing that peo-ple can build on.

REFRESH REGULARLY. Like the contents of a refrigerator, what's up on the board usually goes bad in about a week. Then it's time to erase and start over.

Be alert for good ideas that cross your field of view. The more ideas you brush up against, or even butt heads with, the more you can give yourself the venture capitalist's leverage of seeing a lot of ideas so that you invest in only the very best. Create an eclectic portfolio of short- and long-term ideas, with varying potential for risk and reward. Keep track of them in a folder on your digital device or post them on your wall.

Ask yourself, what can you do to increase your "deal flow" of new ideas? When was the last time you took a class? Read some unusual magazines or blogs? Listened to new kinds of music? Traveled a different route to work? Had coffee with a friend or colleague who can teach you something new? Connected to "big idea" people via social media?

To keep your thinking fresh, constantly seek out new sources of information. For example, we watch dozens of TED Talks a year, scan our favorite news aggregator every morning, and subscribe to expertly curated newsletters like *Cool News of the Day*. We also have more than six hundred IDEO folks in seven countries selectively sharing new ideas they think are "too good to miss." If all that sounds overwhelming, it's not. Once you've found the right data streams for you, it can be incredibly energizing.

Another place to find inspiration is to look for new ideas from different cultures or different kinds of organizations. This kind of cross-pollination between departments, companies, and industries can be particularly useful for individuals who have been working at the same job for a while. Even if you have kept up with the industry blogs and trade publications or studied up on the best of class, it's hard to gain competitive advantage if you and your competitors are consuming all the same data. So why not keep an eye out for new sources of information and learning?

The head of the pediatric intensive care unit at London's Great Ormond Street Hospital got inspiration from watching a Formula One pit crew on television. He was amazed at the precisely sequenced performance of the well-orchestrated team as they serviced a race car in a matter of seconds. In contrast, the hospital had been struggling with chaotic patient handoffs from surgery to the intensive care unit. So he took the extraordinary step of asking a Ferrari pit crew to coach hospital staff members.

The doctors and nurses translated the pit crew's techniques into new behaviors. For example, they now map out tasks and timing for every role in order to minimize the need for conversation. And they step through a checklist to relay key patient information. As reported in the *Wall Street Journal,* the Ferrari-inspired changes reduced technical errors by 42 percent and information errors by 49 percent.

When ideas are in short supply, it's tempting to become possessive or territorial and limit your options. If you have only a few ideas in your idea bank, you're more likely to settle on one of the few you have and defend it fiercely, even if it's not optimal. But when ideas are plentiful and easy—if you (or your team) have a dozen a day—then there's no need to become territorial about them. And if an idea you had gets blended with others, it's not a problem. The whole group shares the credit. After all, there are more ideas where that one came from. Business guru Stephen Covey called this attitude an "abundance mentality," and if you or your team has one, you'll find it much easier to go from blank page to insight.

As Sternberg says, you can choose to be creative. But you have to make an effort to stay inspired and turn creativity into a habit.

ENGAGE RELAXED ATTENTION

Daydreaming gets a bad rap. Watch a classroom scene in nearly any Hollywood movie, and you're likely to see a kid getting busted for daydreaming in class—gazing out the window or staring off into space when the teacher calls on him. It's a case of art imitating life because our minds do tend to wander. But a wandering mind can be a good thing. Researcher Jonathan Schooler of the University of California, Santa Barbara, believes that our brains are often working on "task-unrelated" ideas and solutions when we daydream. That could explain studies showing that prolific mind wanderers score higher on tests of creativity. And new research on the network of the brain similarly found that our minds make unlikely connections between ideas, memories, and experiences when we are at rest and not focused on a specific task or project.

We believe deeply in the problem-solving power of daydreaming. Sometimes it helps to stop focusing so intently on an issue and aim for what David's mentor Bob McKim used to call "relaxed attention." In that mental state, the problem or challenge occupies space in your brain, but not on the front burner. Relaxed attention lies between meditation, where you completely clear your mind, and the laserlike focus you apply when tackling a tough math problem. Our brains can make cognitive leaps when we are not completely obsessed with a challenge, which is why good ideas sometimes come to us while we are in the shower, or taking a walk or a long drive. David often places a whiteboard marker in his shower so he can write a passing idea on the glass wall before it slips away.

So if you find yourself stuck on a problem, take twenty minutes or so off the grid; let your mind disengage temporarily. You may find a solution arriving like a flash of insight.

GETTING INTO RELAXED ATTENTION

When you are stuck on a problem, here are a couple of ways to defocus your mind:

Try taking a walk, away from traffic or intrusions. Poets, writers, scientists, and thinking people of all sorts throughout history have found inspiration while walking. Philosopher-poet Friedrich Nietzsche said, "All truly great thoughts are conceived by walking." Perhaps it is because of the increased blood flow from the exercise, or the emotional distance gained by walking away from a semi-urgent issue that has been occupying your mind all day. A "thought walk" can take place any time of day or night.

Another opportunity to tap the power of relaxed attention occurs each morning. And you don't even have to get out of bed. When you are awakened from a deep sleep, such as when your alarm goes off, you may find yourself in a half-conscious state between waking and dreaming, which is a perfect moment for relaxed attention. We've used this half-dreaming state to come up with any number of new solutions and fresh ideas. And you can, too. Repurpose that snooze button on your alarm. Start thinking of it as a "muse button," so that you leverage those first precious moments of the day. Try it a few times: When your alarm goes off, just press the muse button, and for the next five minutes, let your brain wander in a state of relaxed attention, working in an unfocused way on some challenge or problem that you have been wrestling with. With a little practice, you'll be able to discover some fresh insights before your day even begins.

EMPATHIZE WITH YOUR END USER

In organizations with millions of customers, or in industries serving the broad public, there is a temptation to stereotype or depersonalize customers. They become numbers, transactions, data points on a bell curve, or parts of a composite character built on market segmentation data. That type of shortcut might seem useful for understanding the data, but we've found that it doesn't work well when designing for real people.

The notion of empathy and human-centeredness is still not widely practiced in many corporations. Business people rarely navigate their own websites or watch how people use their products in a real-world setting. And if you do a word association with "business person," the word "empathy" doesn't come up much.

What do we mean by empathy in terms of creativity and innovation? For us, it's the ability to see an experience through another person's eyes, to recognize why people do what they do. It's when you go into the field and watch people interact with products and services in real time—what we sometimes refer to as "design research." Gaining empathy can take some time and resourcefulness. But there is nothing like observing the person you're creating something for to spark new insights. And when you specifically set out to empathize with your end user, you get your own ego out of the way. We've found that figuring out what other people actually need is what leads to the most significant innovations. In other words, empathy is a gateway to better and sometimes surprising insights that can help distinguish your idea or approach.

You can use this kind of anthropological research in the field to gather inspiration at the beginning of a project, to validate concepts and prototypes generated throughout the design process, and to rekindle momentum when ideas or energy are running low. At IDEO and the d.school, we like to observe people in their homes or where they work or play. We watch them interact with products and services. Sometimes we interview them to better understand their thoughts and feelings. This kind of hands-on research can even change your understanding of who the end user is, as it did for the Embrace team when they changed their approach from designing for hospitals and clinics to designing for rural mothers in their villages.

At IDEO, we hire design researchers with social science backgrounds and advanced degrees in fields like cognitive psychology, anthropology, or linguistics, people who are sophisticated at gathering and synthesizing insights from interviews and observations. But you don't need an advanced degree to get out into the field. Usually every team member on a project at IDEO or the d.school takes part in such fieldwork, because the final concept benefits as a result. Cultural anthropologist Grant McCracken says, "Anthropology is too important to be left to the anthropologists." Everyone can improve their empathy skills with a little practice. You may find you'll get some of your best ideas by doing so.

Many organizations or teams use benchmarking when they want to innovate. They check out what their competitors are doing and pick what they consider "best practices." In other words, without questioning current ways of doing things or seeking new insights, they copy and paste. In 2007, when PNC Financial Services was striving to appeal to younger customers, it could have just followed the competition, hiked up interest rates on its checking accounts by half a percent and promoted them with a marketing campaign. Instead, it created a new kind of account for young people, attracting fourteen thousand new customers in the first two months. PNC's story starts not with benchmarking but with seeking to understand the customers it wanted to attract and then committing to improving its relationship with them.

PNC provides retail banking, corporate and institutional banking, and asset management services to more than six million people across the United States. It was looking to reach a new demographic, "Generation Y," the first generation of digital natives, roughly ranging from college age to their mid-thirties. When the team at PNC started getting to know Gen Yers through interviews, it became clear that while tech savvy and adept at weaving technology seamlessly into their lives, they are far from literate when it comes to banking and managing their finances. Even people who were making more than enough to live comfortably were often overdrawn on their account because they would pay bills before their paycheck went through. And they admitted that they needed help.

The team realized that Gen Y would benefit from tools to better manage their money. With greater control over their assets, customers could save more and not overspend, avoiding overdraft charges. As Mark Jones, the service designer on the project, describes it, "For the person living hand to mouth, struggling with money management, the key is to let things be more visible, let them get access, let them tweak back and forth between accounts very easily."

Bank customers love the idea of avoiding overdraft fees. But it takes courage for a bank to create such products because overdraft fees are a highly profitable part of the industry. At the time, banks were collecting over $30 billion a year in overdraft income, and young adults are especially prone to incurring those fees. But PNC decided to build better long-term customer relationships by supporting healthier financial behavior.

The PNC Virtual Wallet is a family of banking products that

provides customers with digital access to their finances and enables them to have better control of their money. Instead of a ledger, a calendar view helps customers visualize their balance, with estimated future cash flow based on when they get paid and when they pay bills. The view highlights Danger Days, when customers might overdraw their account, so they can reschedule bill payments, promoting better planning. A money slide bar graphically indicates and controls fund allocation between Spend, Reserve, and Growth. With the Savings Engine, customers can set their own rules, such as automatically transferring money to savings when they receive a paycheck.

The new direction has paid off with greater deposit growth, making up for whatever revenue may have been lost from bounced check and overdraft fees. One customer described his experience, saying, "I'm just out of college and have a lot more things going in and out than I can keep track of. With Virtual Wallet, I was able to save some, pay all my bills, and know exactly where all my cash went. I have never felt more in control of my money in my life."

Virtual Wallet was a departure from "business as usual" for PNC. But the confidence to go in this direction came from its customers. By getting to know Gen Y and understanding their needs, PNC gained faith in the long-term success of the product.

When we bring corporate executives to observe, meet with, and even talk to customers, the experience makes a lasting impression. "Rather than developing and then testing, we now begin projects with customers, to incorporate their thinking earlier and more effectively," says Frederick Leichter, the chief customer experience officer at Fidelity Investments.

HYBRID INSIGHTS: EMPATHY IN A WORLD OF BIG DATA

Does empathy research conflict with the trend toward "big data"? It's true that there has historically been a split between quantitative market research and qualitative researchers or ethnographers. But is it necessary to disconnect the human stories from the data? Design researchers have recently begun bridging the gulf with what we call "hybrid insights." It's an approach that integrates quantitative research into human-centered design. Hybrid insights allow us to embed stories in the data, bringing the data to life. It brings the "why" and the "what" together. Hybrid insights can include designing a survey in a human-centered way (for example, by being more thoughtful about how we ask questions and keep people engaged). Or it can mean more rigorous concept evaluation where we test prototypes with a large number of users to see if a certain direction merits more exploration.

Coupling insights based on empathy with analytic confidence within relevant target markets may be a way to take the best of both research approaches. So while we're sure the big data trend will continue to grow, decision makers should be careful not to forget about the underlying human element.

DO OBSERVATIONS IN THE FIELD

Observing people in their natural habitat can be difficult—particularly for those who think they're experts already. If you work at a big pharmaceutical company, for example, you probably already know how people take their medicine, right? Empathy means challenging your preconceived ideas and setting aside your sense of what *you think is true* in order to learn what *actually is true*.

While working with Swiss housewares company Zyliss on a line of twenty-four handy kitchen tools, our team at IDEO conducted field observations of people using everyday items like ice-cream scoops. We could have sat at our desks imagining that people use the tools exactly the way we do. We might have designed an ergonomic handle or a smooth scooping action. But when we spent time with people in the kitchen, we saw customer behaviors that pointed to other, less obvious needs. After using the scoop, a number of people absent-mindedly licked the ice cream off the scoop before putting it in the sink. We realized that a really great ice-cream scoop would not only be good at getting ice cream out of the carton, it would also lend itself to licking off that last bit of ice cream when you were done with the job. So we set out to make a "mouth-friendly" scoop. For starters, that meant ensuring no sharp edges or moving parts that a tongue could catch on.

> Empathy means challenging your preconceived ideas and setting aside your sense of what you think is true in order to learn what actually is true.

We could have simply asked people how they use an ice-cream scoop. But they probably wouldn't have mentioned licking the scoop, and might have even denied it. In other words, field research entails more than simply asking people what they want. And it doesn't absolve you of the need to generate good ideas. But it does help you get at latent needs, the non-obvious ones that people aren't conscious of. An interview won't give you that. Sometimes you need to follow consumers into the kitchen.

We learned a similar lesson in a project about the future of beauty care. While the target market was young women, design researchers also went further afield to find the "extreme users"— people at the edges of the normal distribution curve. Extreme users often have exaggerated desires and behaviors that point to nascent needs in the mainstream market, and the unexpected findings from observing them can provide insights and inspiration. One extreme user our researchers interviewed was a forklift driver who claimed he never did anything to take care of himself. As we talked with him, a client team member noticed a foot spa on the floor next to where the driver was sitting. So she asked whose it was. It turns out the foot spa was what he called his "little therapy." He'd soak his feet in hot water and Epsom salts to help with corns and bunions he'd get from his work boots. It turned out that he also regularly got pedicures and used a special foot cream. Without having visited his home, we never would have discovered those behaviors. Observations in the field are a powerful complement to interviews, turning up surprises and hidden opportunities. When you spot a contradiction between what you see and what you expect, it's a sign that you should dig deeper.

When you start looking for these latent needs, you will see them everywhere. A few years ago, Tom found himself on a Japanese train platform in Shinjuku Station, along with colleague and author Kara Johnson. Shinjuku is the busiest railway station in the world, with more than three million people passing through its turnstiles every day, a mix of shoppers, students, and white-collar "salarymen."

Kara and Tom noticed that the young Japanese woman in

Mismatched footwear: silly idea or business opportunity?

front of them was wearing brightly colored sneakers. What caught their eye was not merely the vibrant color among the millions of black shoes in Shinjuku that day. More unusual was the fact that her shoes didn't match. Both shoes had the same contemporary style, but her left shoe was turquoise blue, while the right was a hot pink. What were they seeing? Their first theory was that she owned another pair of shoes almost exactly like those at home—but with the turquoise shoe on the right, of course. Theory number two was that she had a girlfriend with the same shoe size. But theory number three was the most intriguing: that there was a market opportunity for selling mismatched footwear.

Tom was sorely tempted to reject that "silly" idea out of hand. What he didn't realize at the time, however, was that there was already a thriving business around the concept of mismatched socks. A company called LittleMissMatched sold them, with the slogan "nothing matches but anything goes." Its revenues grew from $5 million to $25 million in three years during its initial startup, and it has continued to be successful ever since. So why not shoes? The next time you see something quirky, keep an open mind. You might discover a business opportunity hidden in plain sight.

No matter how high you rise in your career, no matter how much expertise you gain, you still need to keep your knowledge and your insights refreshed. Otherwise, you may develop a false confidence in what you already "know" that might lead you to the wrong decision. Informed intuition is useful only if it is based on information that's accurate and up to date.

Tom had a humbling reminder of the dangers of out-of-date knowledge several years ago when Singapore's deputy prime minister Tony Tan (now president) invited him to participate in a think tank called the Islands Forum. Back in 1985, Tom had spent most of a year living in Singapore while working with the highly respected Singapore Airlines. Any spot in the entire country was within a twenty-mile radius of his apartment, so it was easy to get to know the place very well.

When the invitation from Tony Tan arrived at Tom's office, he started looking forward to the journey. He recalled some of his favorite haunts and how much he enjoyed being immersed in Singapore's culture. But within five minutes of stepping off the plane at the ultramodern Changi Airport, Tom was struck by an embarrassing realization: he didn't know Singapore at all. What he knew and remembered was Singapore 1985—which didn't really exist anymore. Singapore had evolved continuously since the day he'd left. The open-air food stalls at Rasa Singapura—the best street food he'd ever tasted—had vanished, along with the chance to grab a dinner of chicken satay for only two dollars. The new Mass Rapid Transit system, which had been a massive construction site when he lived there, now crisscrossed the city with fifty stations. And it seemed like half the hotels were either new or under new ownership since his last visit. Having learned the "Singapore 1985" lesson during that trip, Tom has tried to remember it ever since.

As the American writer Mark Twain said a century ago, "It's not what you don't know that gets you into trouble, it's what you know for sure that ain't so." Don't be fooled by what you "know for sure" about your customer, yourself, your business, or the world. Seek out opportunities to observe and update your worldview.

ASK QUESTIONS, STARTING WITH "WHY?"

One of the best ways to accelerate learning is to ask questions. A question that starts with "Why" or "What if" can brush aside superficial details and get to the heart of the matter.

Doctors regularly ask their patients questions in order to diagnose illness. But adding a "why" or "what if" approach could improve a diagnosis—and potentially affect treatment. Amanda Sammann is a surgeon who recently joined IDEO as a medical director. It's easy to picture her expertly assessing patients' conditions and swiftly making diagnoses as she exudes the characteristic self-assurance of an experienced physician. So when it came time to do fieldwork in a hospital for her first design project, Amanda told us that she felt like she was on familiar ground.

Coming off a night shift, she had her scrubs and badge on when she joined her teammate for an interview with a young patient. "I walked into the room and said, 'Hello, I'm Dr. Sammann. Tell me about your condition,'" says Amanda. She has talked to patients this way for years, using the textbook language of a clinician. Her teammate gently stepped in, took a seat next to the boy, and started to engage him in a casual conversation about the game he was playing on his phone. As Amanda watched, the boy opened up, eventually talking not only about his disease but also about his family, his day-to-day life, and how he felt about his doctor and his medication. Amanda realized that she usually conducts a completely different conversation, one that builds patient histories and treatment plans rather than establishing empathy.

"When I get into the hospital, it's hard not to go to my traditional role," Amanda says. "But by approaching the interview from a different perspective, we learned so much and got so much farther than we would have with my usual pointed questions."

Amanda is a quick study and was eager to apply what she had learned the next time she got called to the emergency room. Her next patient was an elderly woman who had broken her wrist three weeks earlier. Yet when Amanda saw her, the wrist was still swollen and purple. Clearly she hadn't gotten treatment, and the daughter who had brought her in was furious. Normally after Amanda had examined an injury and recorded the treatment history (or in this case, the lack of treatment history), she would have moved on to her recommendation to follow up with a hand surgeon. But she sensed that something else in the room was broken besides the patient's wrist.

"Generally I would say friction between family members or frustration with mom needing care is not part of your job as a health care provider," she says. However, this time Amanda paused to imagine the "nonsurgeon" approach to this visit. So she asked the patient about herself, and learned the woman was an energy healer. Her friend had performed energy healing on her wrist, and she had seen some improvements, which is why she hadn't gone to the doctor. So Amanda adjusted what she said next in a way she never would have done without that insight into her patient's reasoning. Acknowledging that energy healing has a role to play, Amanda explained that in the case of fracture, a medical doctor was necessary because she risked losing flexibility in her wrist, which would prevent her from practicing energy healing in the future.

Switching from thinking like a surgeon to thinking like an anthropologist led Amanda to connect with her patient in a deeper way. Doing so allowed her to understand her motivations and enabled her to frame the treatment in context. Think about how you approach clients or customers. Do you ask deep, probing questions, or are you hearing what you expect? Are you making a connection or just making contact?

Coe Leta Stafford, a veteran IDEO design researcher with a PhD in cognitive development, has lots of experience asking questions of potential end users. One way she brings questions to life is by making them playful. Instead of asking "Why do you like this book so much?" she'll turn it into a game: "Pretend you wanted to convince a friend that they should read this book, what would you tell them?" She reframes the question in a way that sidesteps some of the "business as usual" responses and elicits more meaningful answers.

Even challenging questions can be framed in ways that help get past cultural or "political" barriers. For example, when Coe Leta wants to understand where an innovative approach might encounter in-house resistance, she suggests, "Imagine you have an 'invincibility' coat that lets you overcome challenging processes or people. Where or when would you use this coat?" The right question can make all the difference.

INTERVIEW TECHNIQUES

One misconception about empathy is that it means going to your customers, asking them what they want, and then giving them exactly what they asked for. That strategy usually doesn't work well. People often lack the self-awareness (or the vocabulary) to express their needs. And they seldom consider options that don't yet exist in the world.

Empathy is more about understanding *latent* needs, even if people can't articulate them to you. By watching real people and their actions, you can learn things you'd never find out if you asked them straightforward questions alone. Here are a few techniques adapted from IDEO's *Human-Centered Design (HCD) Toolkit*. Try practicing them with a partner before you go out into the field.

SHOW ME

If you are in people's homes, workplaces, or other places they frequent, ask them to show you the things they interact with (objects, spaces, tools, etc.). Take pictures and record notes to jog your memory later. Have them walk you through a process from their daily lives.

DRAW IT

Ask the people you are interviewing to visualize their experience through a drawing or diagram. This can be a great way to debunk assumptions and reveal how people think about and prioritize their activities.

FIVE "WHY'S"

Ask "Why?" questions. Do this in response to the first five answers the person you are interviewing gives you. This forces people to examine and express the underlying reasons for their behavior and attitudes. Even if you think you understand, dig deeper into their (and your own) assumptions.

THINK ALOUD

As they perform or execute a specific task, ask participants to describe aloud what they are thinking about. This helps uncover users' motivations, concerns, perceptions, and reasoning.

Asking questions of a diverse range of people will help you to elicit new responses. For example, try asking unexpected experts. If you make refrigerators, ask a repair shop which part needs to be fixed most frequently. Ask a blind person how they use a smartphone. Ask a biomimicry expert to tell you what people can learn by watching ants. Ask a science fiction writer to think about the future of packaging.

Similarly, ask people around you of different age groups for their perspectives. Sometimes the youngest colleagues or members of your team can offer a new point of view that can advance a project. Seeking a younger "reverse mentor" can be a great way for an experienced executive with years on the job to continue to grow, flourish, and stay abreast of new cultural trends in an area of mutual interest. Reverse mentoring can also be a good way to cut through corporate hierarchy to find fresh ideas from unexpected sources and help counter a company's natural tendency to overrely on past experience. Our reverse mentors have helped us with everything from small tips about the latest smartphone apps to practical advice on how to motivate young team members.

REFRAME CHALLENGES

Sometimes, the first step toward a great answer is to reframe the question. Problem statements often assume that you already know what to look for, that you know the correct solution and that the only challenge lies in figuring out how to achieve it. Before you start searching for solutions, however, step back to make sure you have unearthed the correct question. Great leaders are good at reframing the problem. Considering the future of Cisco's high-end TelePresence system, for example, Cisco CEO John Chambers reframed the obvious question, "How can we improve videoconferencing?" as "How can we provide a viable alternative to air travel?"

Reframing the question can send you off in promising new directions. At IDEO, our teams have designed dozens of precision medical devices and surgical instruments. When doctors complained that their hands became tired using existing dissection tools for sinus surgery, our client asked the question "How can we make the tool lighter?" It's a worthy question and points to a solution that would include substituting materials with a higher strength-to-weight ratio, consolidating multiple parts into one, or specifying a smaller, lighter motor. All were potentially viable options. But we reframed the question as "How might we make the surgical tool more comfortable in the hand during long procedures?" The new question opened up a broader range of possible solutions. Working closely with the com-

The first step toward a great answer is to reframe the question.

pany and its medical advisory board, we redesigned the tool, shifting its center of gravity so that it was more comfortable to hold. The finished tool may even have ended up a few grams heavier than the previous device. But surgeons love it.

At IDEO's Munich office, we call the reframed challenge "Question Zero," since it is a new starting point for seeking creative solutions. Reframing the problem not only gives you more successful solutions but also allows you to address bigger, more important problems. For example, many people think high dropout rates in college occur because students cannot afford to stay. That assumption suggests that the underlying problem is lack of scholarships and financial aid. Studies show, however, that only 8 percent of students drop out for purely financial reasons. Researchers are now finding other factors that play key roles, like academic preparedness as well as intangibles like emotional disengagement and lack of a sense of community.

Without getting at these deeper questions, we cannot hope to solve the deeper problems. Even when you're in a hurry for the answer, reframing the question can be time well spent.

One of the most powerful ways to reframe a problem is to humanize it. For GE's Doug Dietz, reframing his work from designing MRI machines to getting young patients safely and willingly through an MRI scan changed not only the product but his life. And it's not just MRIs that could use a bit of humanizing. If you look around, you will see all kinds of things constructed around machine needs rather than human needs. For example, we are both over six feet tall. Why do we have to bend down on one knee to get a can of soda from a vending machine? Because it's easier for the machine to let gravity drop a can into a bin at our feet than to deliver it waist high into our hands. So the machine wins, and we lose.

Rolf Faste, the former director of the product design program at Stanford for twenty years, used to say, "If a problem is not worth solving, it's not worth solving well." Focusing our energy on the right question can make the difference between incremental improvement and breakthrough innovation. Where innovation happens is often in the "Aha" moment when you realize what the *real* problem or need is—and begin solving for that.

REFRAMING TECHNIQUES

Here are some ways to reframe your problem. Try them and see if they lead you to a better question to answer, one that addresses a human need and sparks more inspiration:

1. **STEP BACK FROM OBVIOUS SOLUTIONS.** Instead of trying to invent a better mousetrap, for example, look at other ways to mouseproof your home. Maybe the mousetrap isn't really the problem.

2. **ALTER YOUR FOCUS OR POINT OF VIEW.** John F. Kennedy charged Americans to "Ask not what your country can do for you—ask what you can do for your country," encouraging us to rethink our rights and obligations. Changing your point of view often means shifting focus to a different stakeholder: to a parent instead of a child, or to a car buyer instead of the car dealer.

3. **UNCOVER THE REAL ISSUE.** Decades ago, Harvard Business School professor Theodore Levitt

observed, "People don't want to buy a quarter-inch drill. They want a quarter-inch hole!" If you only asked questions about drills, you might miss out on the possibility of using lasers to create small precise holes like the ones in some laptop speaker grills.

4. LOOK FOR WAYS TO BYPASS RESISTANCE OR MENTAL BLOCKS. If you try to get people to stop drinking the impure water from the local well in a developing country, you may find villagers responding, "My mother gave me water from this well; are you saying my mother was wrong?" If you want to break with the past, that kind of question has to be completely reframed. Instead, you can show how impure and dangerous their current well water is in contrast to how safe the purified water is. Then you can ask a completely different question to parents anywhere in the world: "Which water would you want your children to drink?" New question, very different answer.

5. THINK ABOUT THE OPPOSITE. Working with the Community Action Project in Oklahoma, IDEO.org co-leads Jocelyn Wyatt and Patrice Martin were struggling with how to gain more involvement from inner-city parents in programs that would help their kids' futures. Faced with participation rates of less than 20 percent, they were racking their brains trying to come up with solutions. But when they approached the challenge from the opposite direction and asked, "What are all the reasons we can't get parents to participate?" (busy lives, transportation issues, child care, etc.), it got all the issues out on the table and pointed to possible solutions. For example, instead of emphasizing that the programs were free, organizers started communicating how valuable the programs were for parents and their children. Flipping the question around can be a useful tool for getting past preconceptions or routine ways of thinking so that you can see the situation in new ways.

BUILD A CREATIVE SUPPORT NETWORK

Creative people are often portrayed as lone geniuses or rugged individuals. But we've found that many of our best ideas result from collaborating with other people. From make-a-thons to multidisciplinary teams, we treat creativity as a team sport. Like many elements of creative confidence, building on the ideas of others requires humility. You have to first acknowledge—at least to yourself—that you don't have all the answers. The upside is that it takes some pressure off you to know you don't have to generate ideas all on your own. David realized this early on when he started enlisting buddies to help with his giant plywood structures for Spring Carnival as an undergraduate at Carnegie Mellon University. He later built our company around the idea of working with friends.

Even if you haven't found the right collaborators yet, you too can build on the ideas of others. Check out creative digital communities. Form an all-volunteer project team that works after hours on an idea that's important to you. Spearhead a creative confidence group that meets once a month for lunch or for drinks after work. In other words, take action to build your own supportive community of innovators.

Keith Ferrazzi, author of the bestselling book *Never Eat Alone,* is a vocal advocate for tapping into the power of personal advisory boards when facing big decisions or issues. And David has had several such advisory boards of his own for a long time. They serve as a source of new information as well as a sounding board that either reinforces or challenges his point of view. It helps inspire confidence when you know that there is a group behind you.

Our mother, Martha, has her own personal advisory board in our hometown—although she has never called it that. She and a group of women from her high school class met at least once a month for decades to share their joys and their challenges. They switched to once a week as they got older. They make no pretense of playing cards or doing anything that might distract them from talking through the issues in their families and their lives. They've shared their hopes and their troubles. Occasionally they've cried and consoled one another. No one could ever have a better board of advisors. Now, sadly, the group of eight "club girls," as they call themselves—all members of the Class of '43—has been reduced to a group of three as members have passed on. But the remaining members still meet for breakfast every Wednesday morning in a local diner to talk about their lives and help each other out.

You may not be lucky enough to convene an advisory board that sticks together for seventy years. But with a group of trusted advisors you can call on at key moments, you may find that you get a valuable give-and-take of ideas and alternatives that's hard to match.

CULTIVATE CREATIVE SERENDIPITY

The muses can be fickle. Gaining a flash of insight is never as easy as switching on a light. Nor is it as straightforward as using the methodology of logic, mathematics, or physics. But you can create an "epiphany-friendly" environment within yourself and your organization to cultivate the seeds of creative energy.

French chemist Louis Pasteur famously asserted 160 years ago that "chance favors the trained mind." In fact, some translations of his original phrase (*Le hasard ne favorise que les esprits préparés*) suggest that he really meant chance favors *only* the prepared mind. The history of discovery is full of creative serendipity. For example, growing up in greater Akron, Ohio (then considered the "Rubber Capital of the World"), we learned in history class that Charles Goodyear discovered vulcanization when he inadvertently spilled a mixture of rubber and sulfur on the stove. Even if it happened that way, there's a lot more than mere luck involved in creating a successful business out of it. Once you've spilled rubber on the stove—which anyone in Akron could tell you would smell up the entire house—you have to take a moment to fully understand your discovery, rather than just frantically trying to clean it up before your wife or parents get home. Goodyear both noticed and understood the significance of his breakthrough, which is partly why there is a multibillion-dollar company named after him.

Successful scientists must have been extremely susceptible to such happy accidents because there are dozens of such stories in the history of science and invention. From penicillin to pacemakers, and from saccharin to safety glass, a lot of discoveries have come into this world because scientists noticed that one of their mishaps or mistakes had turned into a breakthrough. Their success-from-failure stories indicate not only that they were keen observers, but also that they were conducting a lot of experiments to begin with. Goodyear didn't just spill a little rubber on the stove while making dinner. He had been searching for a way to stabilize rubber for years and had tirelessly experimented with different approaches. Maybe Pasteur really meant "Chance favors people who do lots of experiments and then pay very close attention when something unexpected happens." Less quotable, of course, but probably more descriptive of reality.

And this kind of serendipity is not limited to the scientific world. Many new ventures have started with a chance encounter, from striking up a conversation at an industry conference to gaining insight from a fellow passenger on a long flight. So, take the spirit of Pasteur's admonition to heart. Nurture the kind of "prepared mind" that seizes the moment when an epiphany occurs. And then try conducting more experiments, as we discuss in the next chapter: moving from planning to action.

Sometimes, simple changes in perspective can spark new insights. If you let go of what you "know," you can start to

> Nurture the kind of "prepared mind" that seizes the moment when an epiphany occurs.

look at things with fresh eyes—and with more questions than answers. But the real insights come from getting out into the world and gaining empathy with the people whose lives you want to improve.

CHAPTER 4

$L E A P$

FROM PLANNING TO ACTION

If you had met Akshay Kothari or Ankit Gupta in their first week of graduate school at Stanford, they might not have stood out against a background of other aspiring engineers and computer scientists in their class. Both were self-described "geeks"—bright, deeply analytical, and definitely on the shy side. Akshay had majored in electrical engineering at Purdue, and Ankit earned a degree in computer science at the Indian Institute of Technology. They had both studied hard and excelled in their undergraduate work before moving to Silicon Valley.

When Ankit arrived on campus, his course load consisted mostly of programming classes like "Logic, Automata and Complexity" and "Machine Learning." So when Akshay told him about Design Thinking Bootcamp, the d.school's introductory class, it sounded like a fun diversion from the densely technical world of computer science. At first, Ankit admits, he felt a little daunted seeing the proliferation of colorful pixel-like Post-its filling the walls at the school, hearing the cacophony of voices in free-flowing dialogue, and witnessing the fearlessness of students and professors as they messed around with pipe cleaners and glue guns. But soon enough, he was immersed in the class, and what had started as a fun diversion turned into an eye-opening experience. "The new way of thinking about creativity and design freed my mind," Ankit says. "Since there was no single 'right' solution, you could have as many ideas as you wanted and ask 'why?' a lot."

Meanwhile, Akshay also found himself in unfamiliar territory. "It felt unnatural," says Akshay, compared to his engineering lecture classes, where he listened to the professor, read the textbook, and relied on his math abilities alone to solve problems. "I was suddenly thrown into this world that was really interesting but kind of crazy—it was a shock." His first class included a hands-on observation/prototyping/storytelling experience called "the ramen project." Students set out to "design a better ramen experience" in one week, using the human-centered design process. Akshay completed each of the steps but felt he had a lot of room for improvement. "I saw how ordinary the concept I created was compared to all the other design solutions." Akshay says that his idea (a celebrity-endorsed ramen) "was kind of obvious . . . something you might come up with off the top of your head." At the same time, he was inspired by how amazing his classmates' concepts were—for example, a really big straw to slurp up noodles and soup together, and a clever container that made it easier to eat ramen while walking. He was determined to keep at it, and by the next project, he could feel that his ideas were already a little fresher. He started making a stronger link between unmet or latent customer

needs and his proposed solutions. He raced through more iterations to learn from each round. He got better at blending his own
ideas with the diverse viewpoints of his multidisciplinary team.

For both Ankit and Akshay, the empathy part of the design
cycle—understanding a product from the vantage point of the end
user—offered a new perspective. Ankit confides that "before the
d.school, we would never have consulted any humans about our
product." The year before, he had worked on starting a company
with some friends in India and managed not to think about—let
alone talk to—a single potential customer. "We spent almost all of
our energy working on the API—the tool set that other developers
would use to interface with our product," he says with a laugh.

The idea of engaging with users face to face initially made
Akshay more than a little uneasy. On his first design research field
trip for a class project, Akshay did most of his "observation" while
trying hard to be invisible at the back of the local grocery store. "I
was looking around, trying to copy how the other students were
doing it," he says. "I saw empathy as a required part and didn't
understand the value of it yet." By the end of the class, however,
he had witnessed firsthand the power of talking to potential customers to spark new ideas and explore new avenues of thought.

The culmination of Ankit and Akshay's d.school experience
was a course called "LaunchPad," taught by consulting associate professors Perry Klebahn and Michael Dearing. Most design
thinking courses are intense, but LaunchPad shifts the experience into overdrive. During the class, you start a company a real
one—from scratch, and incorporate before the quarter is over. No
small challenge. And the pair confesses that in the beginning they
weren't convinced that they could do it.

In the Darwinian tradition of Silicon Valley venture capital, if you want to enroll in LaunchPad, you first need to pitch a fledging business idea. And if your pitch doesn't make the grade (either on content or passion), you don't get in. Akshay and Ankit kicked around many ideas, but they knew they could move forward with only one. They decided to work on the experience of reading the daily news by creating an application for the then-recently-announced Apple iPad. While some of the other ideas they had generated seemed sexier, the ten-week deadline compelled them to choose one that lent itself to rapid feedback.

After they pitched successfully, they soon grasped just how much of a sprint the class would be and how quickly thought would have to translate into action. Their first assignment: build a functional prototype in four days. "That really pushed us," says Ankit. With no time to waste, they set up camp in a café on Palo Alto's University Avenue. Spending as many as ten hours a day there, they realized that—besides the amazing rent deal—their de facto office came with another powerful advantage for their embryonic business: sitting in that cosmopolitan café, they were immersed in a sea of future customers, all sipping their coffee and *reading the news.*

They started with quick, rough prototypes, getting feedback from café patrons every step of the way. At first, they used a series of Post-it notes to simulate the flow of the user interface for their news app. Later, with actual software mockups on an iPad, it got even easier to gather input. "The iPad had just come out, so people were really curious about it," says Akshay. "We used this to our advantage." He would keep one out on the table, and when a passerby inevitably stopped to ask whether it was in fact an iPad, he would hand it over with the latest prototype version of their app open and then watch them interact with it. "We said nothing," Akshay explains, "just observed what they did. This was huge for us, unearthing usability flaws." To maximize their speed, Akshay led user research while Ankit banged out new software versions to keep up with what they were learning. "On any given day, we would make hundreds of small iterations," says Akshay. "And I'm not exaggerating—we changed everything from interaction patterns to the size of a button." The process worked: "In two weeks, we went from people saying, 'This is crap' to 'Is this app preloaded on the iPad?'"

Ankit and Akshay brought the Pulse news reader app to market after thousands of quick prototypes.

The result of their intense effort, rapid iteration, and relentless action was Pulse News, an elegant news reader launched in 2010 that aggregates stories from both traditional and emerging publishing sources. It was so successful that a few months after launch—while Ankit and Akshay were still students—Steve Jobs showed off Pulse from the main stage of the Apple Worldwide Developers Conference, focusing global attention on the two introverts and their app. Today, Pulse has been downloaded by more than twenty million people and stands as one of the original fifty apps in Apple's App Store Hall of Fame. And recently, Ankit and Akshay accepted an offer of $90 million from LinkedIn for the company they built with design thinking.

Looking back on those first couple months of Pulse, the founders got a lot of things right:

- They started with a "do something" mindset and were not content to merely comply with the standard requirements of their graduate programs.
- They minimized planning and maximized action, knowing that the results of early experiments might quickly render even the best-laid plans obsolete. They started interacting with potential customers right away.
- They prototyped quickly and cheaply, fueling thousands of variations that ultimately resulted in their wildly popular final product.
- They thrived in spite of—maybe even because of—their time constraints, spurred on by necessity to develop creative ideas at a blistering pace.

Those elements in Pulse's story demonstrate how imperative action and iteration are to innovation and creativity, both for individuals and organizations. "I learned that creativity is always in hindsight," says Ankit. "It's not about just coming up with the one genius idea that solves the problem, but trying and failing at a hundred other solutions before arriving at the best one."

To embrace that level of experimentation, don't get stuck in the planning stage. Innovation is all about quickly turning ideas into action. That necessity for getting things moving has its basis—at least metaphorically—in the fundamentals of science. Isaac Newton's first law of motion suggests that "a body at rest tends to stay at rest; a body in motion tends to stay in motion." Newton was describing the motion of objects, but we see his principle of inertia at work in individuals and companies too. Some people remain stuck in place, sitting at the same desks, next to the same people, going to the same meetings, serving the same customers, as a changing industry climate trends away from them. Others move forward, but at a familiar linear pace, sticking to the same multimonth planning cycle, following the same review-and-approval process, or continuing the same workflow steps, even as the world accelerates around them.

To overcome inertia, good ideas are not enough. Careful planning is not enough. The organizations, communities, and nations that thrive are the ones that initiate action, that launch rapid innovation cycles, that learn by *doing* as soon as they can. They are sprinting forward, while others are still waiting at the starting line.

THE "DO SOMETHING" MINDSET

One of the qualities we admire most about people with creative confidence is that they are not passive observers. Even in tough situations, they don't act or feel like pawns or victims. They live in the active voice. They write the scripts of their own lives, and in doing so, they have greater impact on the world around them. While the path of least resistance is usually to coast along in neutral, people with creative confidence have a "do something" mindset. They believe their actions can make a positive difference, so they *act*. They recognize that waiting for a perfect plan or forecast might take forever, so they move forward, knowing they will not always be right but optimistic about their ability to experiment and conduct midcourse corrections further down the road.

John Keefe, a senior editor at Manhattan radio station WNYC, one day heard his colleague lament about how often her mom was left waiting at city bus stops, not knowing when the next bus would arrive. Just pause for a moment, and ask yourself the following question: If you worked for New York City Transit and your boss asked you to solve that problem, how soon would you promise to get a system up and running? Six weeks? Ten? John, who doesn't even work for the transit authority, said, "Give me till the end of the day," converting a colleague's passing comment into a personal mission. Within twenty-four hours, he created a working prototype of a service that allowed bus riders to call in, input their bus stop number, and hear the location of the next approaching bus (even without a smartphone).

To bring the idea to life in such a short time, John had to get creative about using existing services. He bought a toll-free phone number for a dollar per month from Twilio, a service that connects a telephone number to web-based programs. He wrote a small program that sends the bus stop code to the NYC Metropolitan Transit Authority site, accesses real-time location data, and then converts the answer from text to speech. A few seconds later, the caller hears a message like this: "the next bus to arrive at Fourteenth Street and Fifth Avenue heading north is nine stops away." He did all that in a single day. And when we called the number a year later to check it out, John's little hack was still working.

John applies the same fearless attitude to his work at WNYC. "The most effective way I've found to practice design thinking is by showing, not telling," he says. "Rather than explaining what it is . . . I say: 'I can get you results next week.'" WNYC has taken the lesson to heart. In 2008, it partnered with d.school students to generate ideas for a morning news show that was under development. Concepts that were conceived and generated by students in California on Tuesday were tested on-air in New York City that same week.

If John Keefe's empowered attitude sounds like it's uniquely his, don't underestimate the contagious qualities of his creative energy. Just days after hearing John's bus stop story, Tom experienced his own epiphany. He was riding his bike home one evening and noticed that an aging bus stop in the city of Menlo Park had been torn down, replaced with a forest green solar-powered bus shelter. The good news of that civic improvement, however, was tempered by the fact that the bus shelter had been installed in the wrong place. Unlike the old shelter, this one stuck six feet out into a popular walking path that serves as the thoroughfare for a veritable army of young fourth-graders riding their bikes to a nearby grade school. Tom couldn't help thinking that once classes began in the fall, a thousand pounds of green metal sticking halfway into the path would wreak havoc with the grade schoolers' daily commute.

He might have been tempted to simply continue on his way, shaking his head at the mistake and writing the situation off as hopeless because "you can't fight city hall." But with John Keefe's story fresh in his mind, Tom pulled his bike over at the side of the road and snapped a few pictures with his phone. Reaching out to an elected official for the first time in his life, he sent an e-mail to the mayor's office that evening, uncertain whether he'd even hear back. But by 10 a.m. the next morning, the mayor had sent an upbeat response, pulling her public works director into the conversation. And a week later, when Tom was en route to work, he spotted a large crane repositioning the bus shelter into its proper place.

Our point? The first step toward being creative is often simply to go beyond being a passive observer and to translate thoughts into deeds. With a little creative confidence, we can spark positive action in the world. So the next time you start to say "Wouldn't it be great if . . . ?" just take a moment, remember John Keefe, and tell yourself, "Maybe I can finish it by the end of the day."

KEEP A BUG LIST TO FIND CREATIVE OPPORTUNITIES

We are surrounded every day by products that don't work well, services that slow us down, and setups that are just plain wrong: the website that requires ten clicks to accomplish what should take only one or two; the projector that stubbornly resists linking up with your laptop; the machine at the parking garage that makes paying so difficult. Noticing that something is broken is an essential prerequisite for coming up with a creative solution to fix it. Making "bug lists," which Tom described in *The Art of Innovation,* can help you to see more opportunities to apply creativity. Whether you use a piece of paper in your pocket or record ideas on your smartphone, keeping track of opportunities for improvement can help you engage with the world around you in a more proactive way. The running list can serve as a useful source of ideas when you're looking for a new project to tackle. Or you can make a bug list on the spot.

Write down the things that bug you, and you'll start being more mindful of them. It may seem like you're focusing on the negatives, but the point is to notice more opportunities to do things better. And while many of the items on your bug list may be things you won't be able to fix, if you add to it regularly, you'll stumble onto issues you *can* influence and problems you can help solve. Almost every annoyance, every point of friction, hides a design opportunity. Instead of just complaining, ask yourself, "How might I improve this situation?"

STOP PLANNING AND START ACTING

With a more proactive mindset, you will start to see more opportunities for action around you. But seeing is not enough. You still need to act.

Many of us get stuck between wanting to act and taking action. The uncertainty of the uncharted path ahead can be daunting. Sometimes it feels as if circumstances are conspiring against us, and we find ourselves riveted in place.

In corporate cultures, that hesitation can translate into what professors Bob Sutton and Jeffrey Pfeffer call the "knowing-doing gap": the space between what we know we *should* do and what we *actually* do. It can lead to company paralysis when talk becomes a substitute for action.

After learning about the knowing-doing gap, we began to see it everywhere. For example, we witnessed it firsthand at the Eastman Kodak Company. On a cold spring day in the mid-1990s, an IDEO team traveled to Rochester, New York, for an audience with the Kodak executive team. We found a group of leaders with deep expertise who at least *intellectually* understood that the future of photography was digital.

Looking back, business historians may be tempted to suggest that Kodak's leadership was naïve. But that was not the case. In fact, we had to race to keep up with CEO George Fisher's agile mind. And no one could say Kodak lacked knowledge of digital photography. They had actually invented the digital camera in 1975 and later pioneered the world's first megapixel sensor. Kodak had a head start that should have yielded lasting advantage. So why didn't all that knowledge and first-mover advantage turn into decisive action?

For starters, tradition got in the way of innovation. Kodak's glorious past was just too alluring. Kodak had essentially owned consumer photography for a hundred years, with market share in some segments as high as 90 percent. By contrast, digital ventures all seemed so risky, and Kodak wasn't providing enough "soft landings" for managers willing to take career risks in those new areas. Facing strong global competitors in the digital market, Kodak knew that it would struggle, and fear of failure transfixed the management team.

Caught in the knowing-doing gap, Kodak clung too closely to the chemistry-based business that had been so successful for them in the twentieth century, underinvesting in the digital world of the twenty-first. What we saw at Kodak was not a lack of information but the failure to turn insight into effective action. As a result, one of the most powerful brands in America lost its way.

No company that falls behind the competition is guilty of standing completely still. But sometimes our efforts fail because of the level of commitment to change. "I'll try" can become a halfhearted promise of follow-through rather than decisive action.

The d.school's academic director Bernie Roth demonstrates this idea with a brief exercise that his students say delivers a lasting message. He holds out a water bottle and asks them to try to take it from him. Facing gray-haired Bernie, a fifty-year veteran of the Stanford Design Program, students usually hesitate as they try to grab it from him. Their initial efforts yield nothing. His grasp just grows more ironclad as the strapping twenty-year-olds and powerful CEOs try to wrestle the bottle away from the octogenarian.

Bernie then reframes the exercise. He says to stop *trying* and *just do it*—take it from him. The next person strides forward and successfully wrenches the bottle away. What changed? As Bernie explains it, a subtle excuse lies in the idea of "trying." It's as if today is for attempts, and the real action will happen at some vague future moment. To achieve your goal, to topple the barriers that stand in your way, you have to be focused on getting it done *now*. Or as Yoda, another wise and seasoned change master, put it to Luke Skywalker in *Star Wars*, "Do or do not. There is no try."

Many who have witnessed Bernie's exercise have taken his message to heart. An editor for a prestigious international business journal who had struggled for years to find time for her true passion—writing fiction—was spurred to begin work in earnest on her new novel. A psychology professor planning to spend a year "gathering more information" on his research topic scrapped that plan and initiated a series of workshops to quickly prototype the final version of his work. And a computer graphics researcher who has been dabbling on and off with a music technology project switched from saying "one day . . ." to saying "*today.*" He wrote a proposal and met with an international development foundation that funds music initiatives.

Sometimes despite the determination to jump in, the enormity of an important task can stop you in your tracks, especially at the beginning. Getting started can be hard. The writer faces the blank page; the teacher, the first day of school; businesspeople, the launch of a new project.

Bestselling writer Anne Lamott famously captures this idea in a childhood story from her popular book, *Bird by Bird*. Her ten-year-old brother had been assigned a school report about birds and hadn't started on it until the night before it was due. "We were out at our family cabin in Bolinas, and he was at the kitchen table close to tears, surrounded by binder paper and pencils and unopened books on birds, immobilized by the hugeness of the task ahead. Then my father sat down beside him, put his arm around my brother's shoulder, and said, 'Bird by bird, buddy. Just take it bird by bird.'"

It's hard to be "best" right away, so commit to rapid and continuous improvements.

We both summon that phrase "bird by bird" when confronted by an intimidating task, sometimes actually saying it out loud. Those three words remind us that, no matter how large the chasm, we can narrow the knowing-doing gap one step at a time.

In other words, to ultimately reach a creative breakthrough, you just need to *start,* regardless of small failures that may occur along the way. It's unlikely that your first try at anything will be a success. But that's okay. It's hard to be "best" right away, so commit to rapid and continuous improvements. The messiness of such trial and error may seem uncomfortable at first, but action allows most of us to learn at a faster rate; it's almost a prerequisite for success. Otherwise, the desire to be best can get in the way of getting better.

This lesson was brought to life for us in a story from the insightful book *Art & Fear*. A clever ceramics instructor divided his pottery class into two groups during the first session. One half of the students, he announced, would be graded on *quality* as represented by a single ceramic piece due at the end of the class, a culmination of all they had learned. The other half of the class he would grade based on *quantity*. For example, fifty pounds of finished work would earn them an A. Throughout the course, the "quality" students funneled their energy into meticulously crafting the perfect ceramic piece, while the "quantity" students threw pots nonstop in every session. And although it was counterintuitive to his students, you can guess how his experiment came out: at the end of the course, the best pieces all came from students whose goal was quantity, the ones who spent the most time actually practicing their craft.

It is a lesson applicable to a much broader range of creative endeavors: if you want to make something great, you need to start *making*. Striving for perfection can get in the way during the early stages of the creative process. So don't get stuck at the planning stage. Don't let your inner perfectionist slow you down. All the overplanning, all the procrastinating, and all the talking are signs that we are afraid, that we just *don't feel ready*. You want everything to be "just right" before you commit further or share something with others. That tendency leads us to wait rather than act, to perfect rather than launch.

When we tell the people we teach or work with to be "sloppy," to do a quick experiment instead of polishing, it makes them uneasy at first. Our colleagues and students tell us that they have to remind themselves that the front end of innovation is supposed to be messy. But it can be liberating in the long run. You might be surprised by how well the process works—and by how good it can feel.

Another behavior that holds us back is procrastination, a failing that seems universal to the human condition. But we've both been inspired by what author Steven Pressfield calls the "war of art." In his book of that title, Pressfield not only captures the essence of procrastination but also gives new hope of beating it. Part of the trick is that he seldom even uses the word "procrastination." He speaks, instead, of *Resistance*. "Most of us have two lives," says Pressfield. "The life we live, and the unlived life within us. Between the two stands Resistance . . . Late at night, have you experienced a vision of the person you might become, the work you could accomplish, the realized being you were meant to be? Are you a writer who doesn't write, a painter who doesn't paint, an entrepreneur who never starts a venture? Then you know what Resistance is."

Pressfield's sleight of hand, substituting the word "resistance" for "procrastination," is more than just semantics. In giving the phenomenon a different name, Pressfield redefines the enemy. Procrastination seems like a form of personal weakness. But Resistance is a force we can do battle with. Mentioning procrastination is a reminder of our failings. But invoking Resistance is a call to arms. It's an obstacle we are challenged to overcome.

There are dozens of reasons why our plans do not come to fruition. Too often tasks get left simmering on the back burner until they evaporate completely. It is easy to let inertia, distraction, and fear keep you from getting started on an endeavor.

Perry Klebahn tells business professionals in the d.school's executive education program, "Don't get ready, get started!" What project, initiative, goal, or dream has been stymied by your own internal Resistance? What can you do *today* to begin to make it happen?

ACTION CATALYSTS

Sometimes you need to give yourself a little nudge. To get over the natural propensity for inaction, figure out what is holding you back and tackle that in some way. Here are some catalysts we use to get started:

1. **GET HELP.** Hire somebody or recruit a willing colleague for a short period to help you. Make your problem someone else's for a while; share the burden to see if they—or you—come up with a new way to make progress.

2. **CREATE PEER PRESSURE.** David has found that he needs someone else in the room to get started. Even if the person doesn't give feedback or add ideas, they provide social pressure to make David show up, the first step to getting something done. For example, using a personal trainer helps motivate David to go to the gym. Even when he's not feeling energetic, he still turns up for his workout because he has made a commitment to his trainer.

3. **GATHER AN AUDIENCE.** Find an attentive listener to move an idea out of your head and into the real world. Talk your ideas through to get your creative juices flowing. And if your audience can give

---

you feedback or food for thought, that's an added bonus.

4. DO A BAD JOB. Suspend judgment of how well you are doing it. Just get something out there. We've found over the years that one way to get traction at the beginning of an innovation project is to write the "bad ad" first: a quick, sometimes even corny advertisement that describes whatever the finished product will be.

5. LOWER THE STAKES. If the problem you are working on feels so important that everything hinges on it, make it less important. Thinking of the perfect place for your team's next offsite meeting might paralyze you with indecision. But if you just list a dozen possible places, you might have the "perfect" location before you know it.

USE CONSTRAINT TO FUEL CREATIVE ACTION

Athough "creative constraint" sounds like an oxymoron, one way to spark creative action is to constrain it. Given a choice, most of us would of course prefer a little *more* budget, a little *more* staff, and a little *more* time. But constraints can spur creativity and incite action, as long as you have the confidence to embrace them.

When we talk to executives about implementing new innovation processes in their organizations, they often don't seem to know where to start. But if we ask them what they could do in a week with a shoestring budget, you'd be amazed at the great ideas they come up with. After an executive education workshop, a vice president at Fidelity Investments told us he was going to try a crazy time constraint on his next project to open up thinking and force rapid iteration. The kickoff meeting for a six-month project was the following Monday. In the "business as usual" schedule for a new web-based customer offering, his team would have roughly two months of planning, two months of making wireframes (outlining the basic page layouts, navigation, functionality, etc.), and two months of preparing the customer-ready version. This time would be different. "When my team meets on Monday," he said, "I'm going to tell them we have *today* to do the whole project." And at the end of the day, he planned to give the team "extensions" of a week and then a month. He was confident that if they spent more time iterating through many ideas rather than trying to plan for a perfect one, the finished product would be more robust and more innovative.

> Constraints can spur creativity and incite action, as long as you have the confidence to embrace them.

A few boundary conditions can spur more creativity, not less. How long would Akshay and Ankit have taken to launch a product without the "impossible" ten-week time constraint imposed by their class? John Keefe gave himself just a day, which forced him to do some scrappy hacking, using services and tools that already existed in order to get it done. Constraints also help when framing challenges, as we discussed in the last chapter.

Francis Ford Coppola, the famous director of both blockbusters like *The Godfather* and spartan "indie" films, recognized the benefits of constraints. "The lower the budget for my film, the more chances I can take," Coppola explained when he and Tom crossed paths one day in Buenos Aires. He described a recent lean, low-budget film project that sparked huge creative energy in his production. During one scene set in Malta, the screenplay called for a right-hand-drive taxi (since they drive on the left there). But Coppola was filming in Romania, where all the available taxis had steering wheels on the left side. In a big-budget movie he'd simply have requested a vintage right-hand-drive taxi and had it flown in from Britain. But a passionate director financing his own movie must be more creative. Coppola asked the makeup team to part the actors' hair on the opposite side for that day of shooting. He then asked the props team to make up a taxi top light and a license plate printed backwards. When the cameras rolled, he shot the entire scene and then later simply reversed the image. We doubt that a single filmgoer noticed his clever—and ultra-low-cost—"special effect."

So try embracing architect Mies van der Rohe's maxim: "Less is more." What constraints make your job "impossible"? Can you use those constraints as a source of creative license, as permission to think differently?

Here are a few ways to use constraints to leap into action:

1. TACKLE A "DOABLE" PIECE OF THE PROBLEM. To get under way, work on the easiest part first. One technique we use for finding the easy part of a challenge is by constrained voting. At the end of a brainstorm or ideation session, there may be a hundred ideas represented by Post-it notes covering the wall. Instead of simply voting for our favorites—usually done by sticking a colored dot on them—we sometimes focus our attention on the bite-sized

chunks. For example, the project leader will say "Put a dot on the ideas you could explore within the next two hours" or "Pick ideas that you could prototype by the end of the week." We constrain our options by looking at how we can make progress *right now*.

2. **NARROW THE GOAL.** Curing world hunger is too big. Set smaller, achievable goals you can act on. Work in a soup kitchen in your local community. Sponsor a child in Cambodia. Narrow the scope until you can see how to get started.

3. **CREATE A MILESTONE (AND CONNECT IT TO A SOCIAL CONTRACT).** When we work on a long innovation project, it helps to build in a series of check-in sessions, peer reviews, and interim milestones to create a "drumbeat" of activity. Project teams tend to experience a surge of enthusiasm and productivity whenever a deadline looms. So instead of establishing one big deadline, build in as many "mini-deadlines" as possible to keep the team's energy up throughout. We risk losing focus in the middle of a three-month project. But if you set up a phone call every Tuesday with your peer advisors or a quick presentation every Friday with the client/decision-maker, you get more than twenty peaks of intensity rather than just one.

So if you're working on a big presentation, schedule a walk-through or a dry run with your team a few weeks before. This live prototype will show what's working and what's not. Then schedule a second "dress rehearsal" the week of the presentation.

EXPERIMENT TO LEARN

What's the best way to make progress toward your goal? In our experience, it's to build a prototype, an early working model that has become a key tool of design thinkers. If you show up at a meeting with an interesting prototype while others bring only a laptop or a yellow pad, don't be surprised if the whole meeting is centered on *your* ideas.

The reason for prototyping is experimentation—the act of creating forces you to ask questions and make choices. It also gives you something you can show to and talk about with other people. We often build physical prototypes. But a prototype is just an embodiment of your idea. It could be an array of Post-its to simulate a software interface, like the ones Akshay and Ankit made when they first started developing Pulse. It could be a skit in which you act out a service experience, such as visiting the emergency room at a hospital. Or it could be a quick version of an advertisement describing a product or service or feature that doesn't yet exist.

Some failure is unavoidable. So you need to relentlessly seek out clever new ways to create low-cost experiments. The best kinds of failures are *quick, cheap,* and *early,* leaving you plenty of time and resources to learn from the experiment and iterate your ideas. There's an art to prototyping in deciding what to create and how rough it should be. If you're interested in whether the flow of a piece of software makes sense, you may just need simple wireframes of each step—quick hand-drawn sketches of screen layouts. But if you have questions about the feeling the experience evokes, creating a screenshot with the right styling may be more important. Eric Ries, author of *The Lean Startup,* calls such a prototype a minimum viable product, or MVP—representing the least amount of effort needed to run an experiment and get feedback.

Several years back, an IDEO team wanted to illustrate new electronic features for a luxury European car company. The automaker was planning to build intelligence into both the key and the car, and the team wanted to demonstrate how the driver's enhanced experience would look and feel. First, the team filmed someone driving an existing car while acting out the new interaction. Then, using a combination of quick physical props and simple digital effects, they made the new features come alive. The finished video clip simulated the appearance and functionality of a future dashboard with new digital displays and interactions.

The result was nothing like the sophisticated special-effects wizardry you'd see from Industrial Light & Magic. But it only took a week to create, and it captured the team's vision well enough for the car company's executives to decide whether the feature set was headed in the right direction. "I love this idea," one of them said. He didn't mean the new features, but the process for testing it. "Last time we did something like this, we built a full system into a dashboard, spent many months and almost a million dollars. Then we took a video of it. You skipped the car and went straight to the video," he said with a laugh.

Besides speeding up that process of experimentation, prototypes are easy to throw away when they fail. Creativity requires cycling lots of ideas. The more you invest in your prototype and the closer to "final" it is, the harder it is to let go of a concept that's not working.

Prototyping quickly and cheaply also allows you to keep multiple concepts alive longer. So instead of making a big bet on one approach based on gut feeling (or what your boss says), you can develop and test multiple ideas. When you do pick a direction, you will be making a more informed decision, increasing your chances of success in the end.

Multiple alternatives also encourage good, honest feedback about your ideas. If you go in with only one prototype, it limits your options. With multiple prototypes, you can have a frank discussion about the relative strengths and weaknesses of each.

THE ONE-HOUR PROTOTYPE

People let potentially great ideas slip away every day. Sometimes we assume that acting on them would take too long or require too much effort. Other times we fail to convince our boss or key stakeholders with words alone. Experiments are one way to lower the bar in trying out an idea. And the faster the experiment, the more likely you are to try.

Just how quick is a rapid prototype? Sometimes time is very short, and every minute counts. Not long ago, toy inventor Adam Skaates and gaming expert Coe Leta Stafford were halfway through a project with Sesame Workshop to develop Elmo's Monster Maker—an iPhone app that leads young children through the process of designing their own monster friend. They had an idea for a new dance feature in which kids could guide Elmo through different dance moves in sync with a simple music track. The two were enthusiastic about the idea, but the rest of the team was dubious. So the feature was in danger of being cut from the final product.

An hour before a conference call with Sesame Workshop, Adam and Coe Leta decided to prototype the feature with whatever materials they had on hand. Working quickly, Adam printed out an oversized image of his iPhone using a giant plotter, mounted

A prototype iPhone app, as captured by the webcam.

it on a sheet of foam core, and cut out a rectangular window where the screen would be. He then stood behind the "phone" so his body appeared in the "screen." Meanwhile, Coe Leta set up her laptop in front of the crude prototype, pointing the webcam toward Adam. Putting the camera into record mode, she then moved her hand into the scene, using her finger to simulate how children would interact with the app—like touching Adam on the nose to make him start dancing. From the point of view of the webcam, the iPhone looked almost real, and Adam danced and reacted as he envisioned Elmo would. A single take, a quick edit, and the video clip was sent off to the Sesame Workshop team members just a few minutes before their meeting.

Adam and Coe Leta's quick video was fun and endearing. It was also much more persuasive than just talking about their ideas would have been. They subscribe to Boyle's Law (named after one of IDEO's master prototypers, Dennis Boyle): never go to a meeting without a prototype. Today, if you download Elmo's

Monster Maker from the iTunes store, you'll see the feature they prototyped in an hour that morning. By acting quickly, they won the team over with their creative idea.

A behind-the-scenes look reveals the secret of creating this quick, low-tech prototype.

TIPS FOR QUICK VIDEOS

Our Toy Lab team is a prolific producer of quick videos both for prototyping and for storytelling. They use such videos to communicate new inventions to toy companies all over the world. Over the past twenty years, Toy Lab founder Brendan Boyle has learned that a compelling video doesn't have to be a high-cost, time-intensive product. A cleverly crafted, engaging video clip can make up in authenticity what it lacks in expensive production value.

Here are the Toy Lab's seven tips on how to make a video prototype sing:

1. WORK FROM A SCRIPT. Don't try to wing it. Memorable sound bites stick because you've carefully chosen those words. A well-edited script will save time in the end and ensure you cover all of your important story elements.

2. USE VOICEOVERS AS A SHORTCUT. For a fast-paced video, a voiceover is the quickest way to convey meaning or "backstory." Voiceovers also streamline editing because it's often easier to add video footage to spoken audio than vice versa.

3. GET ORGANIZED WITH A SHOT LIST. Think through each shot you want in your video: close-ups, wide shots, still images, and so forth. Make a list and cross them off during your shoot to make sure you don't miss any.

4. PAY ATTENTION TO LIGHTING AND SOUND. If you have anything beyond a shoestring budget, decent lighting and a remote microphone are worthwhile investments. Both will help distinguish your final cut from the average home video.

5. BE MINDFUL OF VISUAL RHYTHM AND PACING. A mix of camera angles and styles helps keep the video moving. Don't stay too long in one camera position; a single take can get stale after a few seconds (unless what's happening is really important for the viewer to follow).

6. GET EARLY FEEDBACK. Show rough edits to people new to the content. See what they notice and where they get lost. Have them point out when they get confused. Look for big-picture feedback—is your message getting across? Check by asking them to summarize the video in one sentence.

7. SHORTER IS BETTER! Think of your video as an elevator pitch rather than a documentary. Most Super Bowl spots are only thirty seconds each. If your video is longer than two minutes, you risk losing an impatient audience. If you are struggling to find a place to cut, try watching the video ten times in a row.

PROTOTYPING A SHARED EXPERIENCE

Good prototypes tell a story, and if you can get the audience to become part of that story, the prototype can be even more persuasive. Take, for example, our collaboration with Walgreens, the largest drugstore chain in America. Tasked with rethinking what it means to be a retail pharmacy in the twenty-first century, the team came up with concepts for making Walgreens a more trusted source of advice and support on health and wellness. One part of the design centered around getting pharmacists out from behind the counter so that they would be more accessible to customers.

To build internal support for the concept, the team con-

A foam core prototype of Walgreen's new pharmacy layout made the concept come to life.

structed an ambitious full-scale prototype made out of foam core. Hundreds of white panels were cut and glued into a simplified three-dimensional representation of the proposed store layout. Taking up an entire floor of a building, the prototype showed off the redesigned space and set the stage for team members to act out new service roles. "The prototype made the new vision of the customer experience so tangible," says a designer on the project. "Walking around in the space made it clear the difference that bringing a pharmacist out front would make." At a fraction of the cost of a full build-out, the prototype gathered consensus for an idea that might otherwise have met resistance, winning crucial executive support that pushed the concept forward to implementation.

In the new Walgreens "health and daily living" store format, internal studies showed that pharmacists quadrupled the number of customers they counseled. That full-scale interim prototype was a pivotal tool for turning the concept into a reality that, three years later, has been incorporated in over two hundred Walgreens stores. And *Fast Company* magazine named Walgreens one of the most innovative U.S. health care companies—for two years in a row—partly because of creative solutions like these.

STORYBOARDING A SERVICE

Whereas products can be prototyped with machine tools or 3D printers, new services are prototyped using other methods. One simple approach is to create the kind of storyboard traditionally used by Hollywood movie makers and Pixar animators to map out the flow of a scene. You portray each step of service delivery and each element of the customer experience with a series of comic-book-like frames showing action and dialogue. Don't worry about your drawing ability—stick figures are fine. The point is to think through the steps and start to make your idea or the experience tangible. Here are some hints for storyboarding your new concept:

- Focus your attention by picking a specific scenario to prototype or an experience to map out.

- Capture each key moment with a quick sketch and caption. We often use individual Post-it notes or sheets of paper for each frame of the storyboard. Separate sheets make it easier to rearrange the order or to add and delete steps. Try not to spend more than half an hour on your storyboard.

- Once you have a first-draft storyboard, write three questions it raises about your idea. List any new issues that emerged. Identify elements of the experience that are still unresolved.

- Find someone to walk through your storyboard with. Watch closely for nonverbal reactions and listen carefully to their responses. Use the feedback to refine your service idea—and your storytelling.

GETTING ON BOARD WITH EXPERIMENTATION

One of the "secret ingredients" in a culture of experimentation is getting your team to defer judgment long enough to let an idea evolve. Sometimes the craziest ideas—what we call "sacrificial concepts"—can lead to valuable solutions. If you suppress those seemingly impractical ideas—critique them too early—you may inadvertently stall out the process that leads to practical innovation.

Here is an example of how openness to experimentation yielded breakthrough innovation recently at Air New Zealand. Because of its relatively isolated location in the Southern Hemisphere, the airline flies some very long routes (including a twenty-four-hour journey from Auckland to London with a fueling stop in L.A.). And if you've ever sat through even a few hours in a coach-class seat, you know that there's plenty of room for improvement. But airlines have been stuck in the not-so-comfortable status quo for a long time, balancing customer satisfaction against factors like seat cost, weight, and passenger revenues. "With the world's longest hauls, we had a greater obligation than any other airline to give passengers more," said Ed Sims, then Air New Zealand's international airline group general manager. "We were in danger of benchmarking ourselves against competitors and just tweaking around the edges."

So Air New Zealand CEO Rob Fyfe challenged his team to rethink the customer experience on its long-haul flights—including the seats. He made it clear that a risk-averse operational culture shouldn't stop experimentation in the commercial and product parts of the business: "I am quite comfortable with making the odd mistake, if it comes in the pursuit of new opportunities and new ideas," Fyfe says.

With license to exercise their creativity, Air New Zealand managers joined forces with our team for a design thinking workshop aimed at generating breakthrough ideas. They brainstormed and prototyped a dozen unconventional (and some seemingly impractical) concepts, including harnesses that hold people standing up, groups of seats facing one another around a table, and even hammocks in the air. Because everyone was actively participating, no one was afraid of being judged. "It was liberating getting on the floor with cardboard, polystyrene, and paper, cutting out seat concepts," said Sims. One concept the team developed was to include bunk beds for passengers to sleep in. Although the idea initially sounded promising, further prototyping revealed the likelihood of awkward and undignified moments whenever a passenger climbed into or out of the top bunk.

By being open to wild ideas and questioning assumptions, they developed the Skycouch. It's a deceptively simple solution to a long-standing pain for passengers: being unable to lie down in economy class. Although it might seem unavoidable that lie-flat seats take up more room (as they do in business-class cabins around the world), Air New Zealand challenged that conventional wisdom with Skycouch. The seats include a heavily padded section that can be swung up like a footrest, transforming a row of three seats into a futon-like platform that a couple can lie down on together. Industry observers have begun referring to the new seating configuration as "cuddle class."

Air New Zealand took some risks in developing their own custom seating and taking such a bold, experimental approach, but their efforts have paid off. The design has earned the company multiple accolades, such as receiving *Condé Nast Traveler*'s Innovation & Design award and being named *Air Transport World*'s Airline of the Year.

LAUNCH TO LEARN

Once you embrace the idea of leaping into action, small experiments become a key source of new knowledge and insight.

Successful companies of every size embrace experimentation in order to stay ahead of disruptive trends and lead market change. It is a way to rapidly test unanswered questions about everything from design details to new business models.

Traditionally, experiments in the business world have happened internally and behind closed doors. But today, innovative companies "launch to learn" in the open market. Instead of waiting until the end of a development cycle, launching is a way to test and gain insights that you can apply to your product as you continue to iterate.

Many startups already have adapted this model. Ever in beta and working on new releases, they do a little bit of design, implement it, launch it, and then make quick course corrections before launching again. When they learn something isn't working, they adjust as rapidly as possible. By launching a series of small experiments in order to learn, they avoid the risk of spending years perfecting one major product—only to find out no one wants it. By making your corporate R&D cycle more iterative, you can continue to learn and innovate after a product ships.

Game-changing investment platform Kickstarter has become a popular way of launching to learn. Allowing entrepreneurs to test the marketability of their idea at a very early stage, it helps answer the question "if you build it, will they come?" Creators make a pitch for funding, and backers from around the world pledge their financial support. If the funding goal is reached by a predetermined deadline, the venture gets funded. Otherwise, the backers keep their money and the would-be entrepreneurs have to try another path. In its first four years, Kickstarter has helped crowdsource almost half a billion dollars for more than thirty-five thousand creative projects. And the votes of confidence from

Kickstarter backers not only provide financial support but also help entrepreneurs confirm whether there is demand for their new ideas before they jump in all the way.

Applying some creative thinking, you can come up with many different ways of launching to learn. For example, social gaming company Zynga uses a technique it calls "ghetto testing" to estimate demand for new game concepts. Before writing a single line of code, it posts a teaser ad for the game on a popular website and tracks the number of potential customers who click on it. Similarly, a few days after Amazon announced a lending feature for Kindle books, an entrepreneurial product manager in Britain set up a Facebook group to gauge interest in matching up book lenders with borrowers. When more than four thousand members signed up, she felt confident enough to create her own lending/borrowing site and went live just two weeks later with what is now Booklending.com.

As IDEO design director Tom Hulme puts it, "Release your idea into the wild before it's ready." Real-world market testing (even when you know you have more development to do) can be an invaluable source of insight.

CREATING INFECTIOUS ACTION

Little changes can eventually add up to a big impact. Starting small gets you from a state of rest to a state of motion, and you've started to build momentum for the bigger challenges ahead

"Creating Infectious Action" was a high-energy d.school class that challenged students to make an idea go viral—or to literally start a movement. Although that may sound intimidating, with some coaching and a few design thinking tools, students were able to prototype everything from grassroots marketing campaigns to entire businesses. They surprised themselves (and sometimes us) with how much impact their ideas could generate.

David Hughes, a former army captain who flew combat helicopters in Iraq and Afghanistan, told us the story of one such project. Seeking to reduce local gasoline consumption, he and a group of students started an initiative to transform downtown Palo Alto into a pedestrian mall. The eight-block stretch of shops and restaurants along University Avenue is often so clogged with traffic that drivers sit in their cars, engines idling, as they watch pedestrians pass them by. By creating "sticky" stories and leveraging their social networks (e.g., asking professors with popular blogs to write about the concept), the students found that the pedestrian mall idea spread like wildfire.

Within two weeks, over 1,700 people signed the petition or joined a Facebook group backing the initiative. The team got the support of the former Palo Alto mayor, and merchants put stickers in their windows. Soon they were invited to City Hall to address the City Council. The idea was never implemented, but the team got a lot further than they imagined, given the constraints of a one-month project.

As an operations-oriented person who never thought of himself as creative, Hughes was inspired by seeing how much power the team had to influence opinions and behaviors. Now teaching at West Point, he told us, "I used to think that to make something happen in a corporation or in the army, you had to be at the higher ranks, to be a general. But you just need to start a movement."

EXPERIMENTING YOUR WAY TO SUCCESS

Whether your resources are abundant or scarce, embracing experimentation can help fuel the fires of innovation. Experiments, by their very definition, are expected to have a higher rate of failure. But if you recast the traditional failure-is-not-an-option attitude as a series of small experiments, you can actually increase your chances of long-term success.

Many years ago, our longtime strategic partner Jim Hackett had a change he wanted to make. Jim is CEO of Steelcase, and he pointed out to his senior team one day that although they were the world's largest maker of system furniture (what Dilbert would call "cubicles"), leaders at the very top of the company all worked in conventional walled offices with doors. Jim could have introduced a dramatic break with tradition by telling them, "Going forward, we are all moving to open offices." In most organizations, such a unilateral shift would have encountered fierce resistance as, one by one, executives requested a private meeting to voice their objections. But Jim is a natural leader, and that's not what he did. Instead, he proposed an experiment. He suggested that—for six months—everyone on the team try moving out into an open-air Leadership Community, equipped with the latest office furniture and technology. "I don't want any foot dragging," Jim said. "I want you to give it an earnest try. And at the end of six months, my promise to you is that whatever's not working, we will make it better." Jim is a leader of very high integrity, and everyone took him at his word. Who could reasonably refuse to participate

> Embracing experimentation can help fuel the fires of innovation.

for just six months? Knowing that there might be hiccups along the way, they trusted that any real problems would be addressed. The result turned out to be a high-energy environment for the team, and even a de facto showcase for visiting executives. Nineteen years later, Jim Hackett and his team are still tweaking their "experiment," but the Steelcase open-air Leadership Community is going strong. Ask members of the executive team today, and they will tell you that they love it—and wouldn't think of moving back.

Our point? Try recasting your changes as experiments to boost reception and increase creative confidence. Some will fail (that's why it's called "trial and error"). But many, protected under the nonthreatening umbrella of experimentation, may raise your chances of success.

MAKING NEWS

With a belief in your own creative capacity, you feel empowered to take action, to become an agent for change in your environment—at work, at home, or in the world at large. As Akshay reflects back on the creation of Pulse News and his journey to creative confidence, he cites his bias toward action as a key way his ideas get better and more innovative. "Most analytical people don't have a bias toward action, including myself formerly," he says. "If I had an idea, I would just keep thinking about it in my head, or I'd talk about it, but I wouldn't do anything about it. Now it feels natural to have an idea and then immediately build a prototype, whether it's in thirty minutes, four hours, or a week. If I'm excited about something, I'll go ahead and do it."

So don't sit back and let circumstances determine your fate. Take action yourself, and influence the actions of others. As one of our favorite radio journalists, "Scoop" Nisker, used to say at the end of every one of his broadcasts, "If you don't like the news . . . go out and make some of your own."

CHAPTER 5

SEEK

FROM DUTY TO PASSION

Anyone who has worked one on one with David has probably seen him dash off this disarmingly simple line drawing: a seesaw, with a heart on one side and a dollar sign on the other. This tension between the heart and the dollar illustrates a big theme in our lives. To us, the heart represents humanity, in the form of personal passion or company culture—happiness and emotional well-being. The dollar sign represents the financial gains or business decisions that keep the lights on. The seesaw is a reminder to consciously pause and consider both aspects in decision making—especially when it comes to career moves that might look good but feel bad.

Back when Tom was a management consultant, he once lamented to a friend who was a social worker how sad it was that his profession got paid so much, while her profession got paid so little. Without a moment's hesitation, she said, "That's because you have to pay people a lot to do management-consulting-type work, but I'd do the social work for free if I could afford to." For her, the heart outweighed the dollar.

And eventually Tom left management consulting to come work with David at IDEO, choosing to follow his heart.

A few years later, Tom received a desperate phone call from his former boss, the charismatic head of the firm's Transportation Practice. They had just won a huge consulting project with a global airline, but a key employee had quit on them unexpectedly. They risked losing millions in revenue if they didn't find a well-qualified replacement—and fast.

"How much are they paying you at that little design firm?" Tom's former boss asked, guessing that money was the most appealing incentive he could offer. When Tom inadvisably gave him an actual number, his ex-boss offered a financial package that would triple it.

Together as brothers we stared at the heart/dollar seesaw for several hours, discussing what we wanted out of life. The opportunity to work together and pursue interesting challenges side by side had huge appeal to both of us. But to Tom, it felt reckless to turn down that much money. On the one hand, the short-term financial gain would be great. On the other hand, he loved working with his brother and found the work at IDEO to be the most engaging of his life. It took Tom a few days to call his ex-boss back and turn down the offer. But he did.

David, too, has made a career out of decisions that optimize for meaning, rather than money. He has walked away from a thriving venture capital firm he founded, declined generous offers of stock options, and turned down the possibility of a lucrative IPO. Meanwhile, he's found great intrinsic reward in building creative confidence among students, clients, and team members.

It's hard to balance on the heart/dollar secsaw. Society places great value on affluence and the privileges of wealth. But if you're like us, you probably know people who went for the money and now feel miserable or trapped. Like the analyst at a well-known investment bank in Manhattan who sticks with her job, ignoring how the stress makes her break out in hives. There's the newly minted MBA who landed an IT job with what he thought of as one of the world's most respected companies but became so disillusioned that he felt life was passing him by. Or the lawyer who spends every weekend catching up on billable hours, rather than catching up with family and friends. That's why, when faced with a trade-off between money and the heart, we believe it makes sense to consider both. Money will always be easier to measure, which is why it takes a little extra effort to value the heart.

Economic research demonstrates that—above a certain threshold—money isn't strongly correlated to happiness. People who live at subsistence income levels may not be able to afford to

> Money will always be easier to measure, which is why it takes a little extra effort to value the heart.

follow their passion and optimize for the heart. But for the majority of us, how can we afford *not* to?

THE "LOOKS GOOD, FEELS BAD" TRAP

The safe and prestigious job that makes your parents smile, impresses classmates at your college reunion, or sounds good at a cocktail party can make you unhappy if it's not a good fit. One person we know attended an Ivy League school on a music scholarship before switching to the study of medicine because being a doctor seemed like a more reliable career choice. Now a practicing physician, he sees medicine as merely a job, not intrinsically rewarding.

Even more people we know chose a profession based on what seemed reasonable, without thinking about other options. They never questioned their career track, since the first day of the job they took right out of school. Now they work ever-longer hours so they can pursue the next promotion, without stopping to examine why they want it. A close friend of ours started literally counting down the days until retirement, even though it was still over a year away.

Researcher and professor Robert Sternberg told us, "People get so bogged down in the everyday trivial details of their lives that they sometimes forget that they don't have to be trapped. It's sort of like those Chinese finger traps you had when you were a kid. The more you tried to pull your fingers out, the more you were stuck. But when you pushed them in, you could get out. Sometimes, you just have to redefine things." No matter what your age, you can still pursue your passions.

As a young adult, Jeremy Utley had excelled at analysis and

critical thinking. His natural talent led several well-intentioned career advisors to tell him, "You need to go into law or accounting or physics or finance." Jeremy followed that line of thinking and wound up in his mid-twenties in a well-paid job doing financial analysis.

Like too many of us, Jeremy found himself trapped by the "curse of competence." Yes, he could successfully perform all the requirements of his job, but he gained no real fulfillment from what he did. Raised with a tireless work ethic, Jeremy showed up at the office every day, "resigned to the fact that I would hate whatever I did for the next twenty years."

His company expected associates like Jeremy to take a break after a few years to get an MBA. So in the fall of 2007, he started at Stanford's Graduate School of Business. While at the GSB, he enrolled in an introductory Bootcamp class at the d.school as a diversion from his traditional business school coursework. Eventually, he realized how much fun he was having in the class—despite how hard he was working—as he struggled to grapple with ambiguity, prototype his ideas, and make creative decisions. "Up until then, I had been writing off the Bootcamp course as 'playtime,'" he says. "I realized halfway through that it was just as rigorous as anything that I had done in the past, but much more rewarding."

He kept taking classes and became increasingly torn between the mindset of the old job and his new way of thinking. Eventually, he decided to leave behind the tempting salary and status of his previous career path, even though it meant paying back his employer for two years of tuition. "I really didn't feel right about going back to the firm because I'd had a transformative experience and felt like I needed to pursue the new path." So he continued at the d.school as a Fellow, eventually becoming a director of executive education. Asked if he had second thoughts, Jeremy says, "No—I feel good about it. There is peace and joy in my home, and that is priceless to me." Today, Jeremy's passion is reflected in his work—he is widely considered one of the best instructors at the d.school.

Jeremy recently noticed that he has stopped using the word "work" to describe the activity that earns him a living. If a friend calls to ask him what he's doing, he says, "I am at Stanford" or "I'm hanging out at the d.school." He almost never says, "I'm at work."

And that's the point. Work doesn't have to feel like "Work with a capital W." You should be able to feel passion, purpose, and meaning in whatever you do. And that shift in perspective can open up a world of possibilities.

BORED AT BOEING

David took a "looks good, feels bad" job right out of college. Graduating with an electrical engineering degree from Carnegie Mellon in the 1970s, he landed an engineering position at Boeing in Seattle working on 747 jumbo jets. The job was considered a great opportunity; Boeing was—and is to this day—considered one of the most prestigious manufacturers in America. Our father worked his entire career in the aerospace industry, so David's job at Boeing sounded good to our parents as well.

There was just one problem: David hated it. He felt lost in a room full of two hundred engineers crouched over drafting tables, toiling away under fluorescent lights. As a mechanical engineer in the "Lights and Signs" group, his biggest project was working on the 747's LAVATORY OCCUPIED sign. It was a position that didn't play to his strengths as a collaborator. Nor did the job feel like a stepping-stone to something he did want to do. So it was a good job in terms of status and pay, but David was bored and deeply unhappy.

The fact that thousands of aspiring engineers would have coveted David's job only made him feel worse. In the end, David quit, hoping that what had been a daily grind for him might lead to a genuinely gratifying career for the next engineer who took over his drafting table.

The contrast between the passion we both feel for work at IDEO and the heavy sense of duty David felt at Boeing is a difference of night and day. Instead of feeling isolated in a room full of strangers, we get to work with friends and family in an eclectic environment that is always engaging and constantly changing. Most important, we are able to bring our whole selves to work—quirks and all—which helps us make a more meaningful contribution.

The "looks good, feels bad" trap is all about avoiding a career that makes you feel unhappy—and finding the right fit in terms of your interests, skills, and values.

A JOB, A CAREER, OR A CALLING

Amy Wrzesniewski, an associate professor of organizational behavior at Yale University's School of Management, has extensively researched working life, surveying people in a variety of occupations. She has found that people have one of three distinct attitudes toward the work they do: they think of it as either a job, a career, or a calling. And the difference is crucial. When work is strictly a *job*, it may effectively pay the bills, but you're living mostly for the weekend and your hobbies. Those who see work as a *career* focus on promotions and getting ahead, putting in long hours to achieve a more impressive title, a larger office, or a higher salary. In other words, you are focused on checking off achievements rather than pursuing deeper meaning. In contrast, for those who pursue a *calling,* their work is intrinsically rewarding in its own right—not just a means to an end. So, what you do professionally fulfills you personally as well. And often that work is meaningful because you are contributing to a larger purpose or feel part of a larger community. As Wrzesniewski points out, the origins of the word "calling" are religious, but it maintains its meaning in the secular context of work: the sense that you are contributing to a higher value or to something bigger than yourself.

But whether you see your work as a job, a career, or a calling depends on how you perceive it, not necessarily upon the nature of the profession itself. In the early 1990s, for example, Tom's wife, Yumiko, worked as an international flight attendant at United Airlines. Having lived most of her life in Japan, Yumi grew up believing that this was a prestigious, cosmopolitan position, and nothing during her time at United shattered that belief. Yes, the job was sometimes very tiring, and the working conditions could be stressful. But she saw herself as a caregiver in the air, helping her passengers have a rewarding flying experience. Tom saw her in action just once, on a Christmas morning, flying out of Seoul. She greeted everyone on the long flight with a radiant smile and zipped around the cabin with tireless energy, pausing to entertain toddlers and chat with business travelers. What others might see as strictly a *job,* full of routines and hassles, Yumi viewed as a way to positively impact the lives of others.

Our point? What matters most about your career or position is not the value that others put on it. It's how *you* view your job. It's about your dream, your passion. Your calling.

IDEO partner Jane Fulton Suri found her calling when she switched from fixing problems to preventing them. Jane had been a researcher identifying design flaws in products that led to injuries and fatalities. She investigated the ways in which lawnmowers hurt those who used them. She explored why car drivers fail to notice approaching motorcycles. She examined the ways that power tools and chainsaws could result in accidents, despite their manufacturers' best attempts to make them safe to use.

After many years of forensic, after-the-fact analysis, Jane became frustrated with arriving at the "scene of the crime" too late to prevent it. So, using the research skills she had honed observing *bad* products, Jane decided to find a position where she could help to create *good* ones. In her new role, she teamed up with designers to create foolproof fishing gear, more comfortable baby strollers, and more intuitive medical devices. The firm was already full of strong technical minds good at figuring out problems. But Jane helped keep users' needs at the heart of every solution. Although the analysis work had been an intellectual challenge, she found the creative work much more emotionally rewarding. And her human-centered designs persuasively demonstrated the value of empathy, embedding it in the DNA of the firm.

Sometimes looking at your field in a new way can make all the difference. But just because you are passionate about what you do doesn't mean it will be easy. Redefining your role may take even more work and perspiration.

Erik Moga, a design researcher at the company Square, once aspired to be a professional euphonium player. As a child, he loved performing onstage with the tuba-like brass instrument. But he *hated* the drudgery and effort of practicing, of playing a piece over and over again to master it. In high school, he saw virtuoso cellist Yo-Yo Ma perform, and he was lucky enough to be one of the handful of students who got to ask the legendary classical musician a question. Erik smiles wryly as he remembers what he asked: "Isn't it wonderful now that you have made it as professional musician that you don't have to practice anymore?"

The question hung in the air for a moment before Yo-Yo Ma delivered the bad news to Erik. Long after ascending to the top of his field, Yo-Yo Ma continues to practice as much as six hours a day. Erik was crushed. But Yo-Yo Ma's lesson is a reminder to us all—passion doesn't preclude effort. In fact, passion demands effort. But in the end, you are more likely to feel that all that effort was worthwhile.

SEEK YOUR PASSION

David initially imagined that the d.school would help law school students become more open-minded lawyers and MBA students more innovative businesspeople. And that has been true. But we've been surprised at times to see former students actually switching their fields as they engaged their creative confidence.

That was what happened with biophysics PhD candidate Scott Woody.

After four years of bench work studying motor proteins and point mutations in DNA, Scott had grown weary of the lab. "I'd work by myself on one thing and maybe occasionally, every couple months, come up for air and talk to someone, but then I'd have to go back," he tells us. "I was like a drone. It felt like there was no room for thinking outside of my narrow focus, and it really started to drag me down." Looking for something to shake him out of his funk, he went in search of inspiration as far from the lab as possible, signing up for courses including an English literature seminar and even a synchronized swimming class. At a business workshop, he heard about our d.school studio class called Creative Gym, aimed at helping people from diverse backgrounds exercise their creative muscles.

Each two-hour class is filled with a fast-paced succession of hands-on exercises that hone foundational skills for creativity: seeing, feeling, starting, communicating, building, connecting, navigating, synthesizing, and inspiring. Activities range from the playful and the seemingly silly (such as making a piece of wearable jewelry out of tape in just sixty seconds) to the extremely challenging (such as expressing a moment of disgust using only squares, circles, and triangles). The goal of the class is to get students more attuned to their intuition and to heighten their awareness of their surroundings.

"I'm a pretty reserved person, but that class was so much fun," Scott says. "It was a chance to be a little weird, to go nuts. It was the highlight of my week, every week. It opened a lot of creative doors that I had left closed for a long time and that my analytical training had kept shut."

After that Creative Gym class, he realized that he was no longer afraid to explore different approaches. He developed a new willingness to try things that he wasn't sure he was good at— experiments that might not work. "So many of us lack the courage to pursue a new idea or skill," Scott says. "Just by taking action you're better off than ninety-nine percent of people." At his lab, he suggested a new format for their weekly meeting. To introduce informal discussion, he asked everyone to prepare a single slide for a succinct update, breaking their norm of having one person presenting an hour-long PowerPoint deck.

He later applied to LaunchPad (the class in which Akshay and Ankit created Pulse News) without any prior experience in entrepreneurship or engineering. Inspired by job-hunting friends, his initial entrepreneurial idea was a tool that helps you create custom versions of your résumé to use in applying for different positions. To increase his chances of getting into the class, he forced himself to go door to door down Main Street in Petaluma, cold-calling business owners to gather insights about their hiring process in order to improve his pitch. "It was so painful," Scott laughs. "One, because most of them didn't want to talk to me, and two, because I was really nervous." After he got into the class, he continued pushing himself to do things he had never done before: presenting his ideas to venture capitalists invited to the class, interviewing potential customers, and rapidly iterating his design.

Scott's newfound creative confidence, coupled with the growing realization that science research was not his true calling, gave him the courage he needed to set out on a bold new path. A year or two away from earning a distinguished biophysics doctorate degree, he decided to step away from the lab, quit his PhD program, and pursue a startup related to how businesses recruit talent. Back home, his parents were less than enthusiastic when they heard the news. His mother felt sure that Scott was making the wrong decision. This was particularly hard for Scott to hear, because he felt that he had to do it anyway, with or without her blessing. A month later, when she saw him in person for the first time since he broke the news, Scott's mom had a change of heart. She could see in his face that her son was happier than he'd been in years. She told him he was doing the right thing. Two years later, Scott is CEO of his own venture-backed startup, Foundry Hiring, which helps companies manage and analyze their recruiting process. Scott says he hasn't looked back: "I thought work was supposed to suck, that work was work. Now I am doing a job that I love and that is fun."

When people like Jeremy and Scott "flip" into a state of creative confidence, their faces light up with newfound optimism and courage as they talk about their new outlook. Some people, like Scott, have been actively unhappy with their work lives for a while. Most of the people we meet, however, aren't fully conscious of their level of dissatisfaction with their work. They just know that they could contribute more, if they were able to approach what they do differently. They realize they are just bringing half of themselves to work.

When people go for the heart—when they seek out passion in their work—they can tap into and unleash inner reserves of energy and enthusiasm. One way to begin accessing this inner reserve is to jot down moments in your life when you feel really alive. What were you doing and who were you with? What about it did you love? How can you re-create key elements in other situations? Once you've identified a few areas you want to explore further, commit to taking a single tiny action each day to broaden your portfolio of creative experiences in those areas.

FIND YOUR SWEET SPOT

One of the most eloquent descriptions we've encountered of the sweet spot between passion and possibility came from Jim Collins, author of bestselling business books *Built to Last* and *Good to Great*. Tom ran into him at a speaking event many years ago just as

Good to Great was hitting the market. In his talk, without a Power-Point or even a whiteboard, Jim began by drawing a Venn diagram of three overlapping circles in the air, challenging the audience to follow along using "theater of the mind."

The three circles represented three questions you should ask yourself: "What are you good at?" "What will people pay you to do?" and "What were you born to do?" If you focus on just what you're good at, you can end up in a job you are competent at but that doesn't fulfill you. As for the second circle, while people say, "Do what you love and the money will follow," that's not literally true. One of David's favorite activities is tinkering in the studio above his workshop; one of Tom's dreams is to travel the world, collecting stories and experiences from different cultures. So far no one has offered to pay us to do those things. The third circle—what you were born to do—is about finding work that is intrinsically rewarding. The goal is to find a vocation that you're good at, that you enjoy, and that someone will pay you to pursue. And of course it's important to work with people you like and respect.

The audience members that day all seemed to have the same burning question: how do you know what you were born to do? We believe the answer is related to what Mihaly Csikszentmihalyi, an expert in the field of positive psychology, calls "flow"—that creative state in which time seems to slip away and you are completely immersed in an activity for its own sake. When you are in a state of flow, the world around you drops away and you are fully engaged.

To find those things that create a sense of flow, Jim Collins used his own unique form of self-analysis. He was a nerd at an early age, and as a child he used to get out a lab notebook and write down his scientific observations. He'd capture a bug, put it in a jar, and watch it for days, recording everything in his notebook about what the bug did, what it ate, and how it moved. As an adult, he landed a good job at Hewlett-Packard, but he felt unsatisfied. So he reached back to a familiar technique. He bought one of those same lab notebooks from his childhood and wrote "A Bug Called Jim" on it. For more than a year, he did a careful observation of his own behavior and work practices. At the end of each day, he'd write down not just what happened, but what made him feel the best about himself during the day. After more than a year of lab notebook entries, a pattern emerged. He felt happiest when he was working on complex systems and when he was teaching others. So he decided he should teach others about systems, and he left HP on a path that led him to academia. Jim found the magic formula for his own success. But his greatest legacy might be helping others find theirs.

RATE MY DAY

As David emerged from his cancer treatments at the end of 2007, he realized that he had literally been given a second chance in life. On the advice of psychiatrist Dr. C. Barr Taylor, David began using a very simple method of examining what his days were like and finding ways to make them better.

Every evening before bedtime, he would reflect briefly on the ups and downs of his waking hours. He would then score the day in terms of how much fun he had, on a scale from one to ten, and mark it on his calendar. After collecting a couple weeks' worth of data, he went back and reflected over his calendar together with Barr to find what activities drove the number up or down.

They discovered some surprising patterns. Days in which David had a solitary hour or two in his studio space—a rustic loft over a barn—were more rewarding, happier days. And his score bumped up even higher when he blasted his favorite music while making something in the studio—whether it was a metal bracelet, a custom piece of wooden furniture, or a papier-mâché Halloween costume. He identified which activities—work related and otherwise—gave him the greatest sense of satisfaction and accomplishment. He also noticed which ones dragged him down. And then he began gravitating toward those activities that raised his scores and away from things that lowered them.

It was a very simple process. But it led David to moments of epiphany and behavior change—articulating new insights he hadn't previously discovered about himself.

So try identifying the things that bring *you* happiness and fulfillment. Look for ways to incorporate more of those things in your life, whether it's helping others, getting more exercise, reading more books, going to a live concert, or taking a cooking class. A designer at IDEO used to place stickers in her appointment book to note moments when she was happy, anxious, or sad. The modern-day equivalent can be easily found with mood-mapping apps that allow you to keep track of your daily ups and downs, so you know what you want to do more of—and what you want to do your best to avoid. This "mood meter" can help you think about both your work and your personal life.

You don't necessarily have to do anything elaborate

to gain some new insight into yourself. Simply take the time to ask yourself each day, "When was I at my best?" or "When was work most rewarding?" It can help point you toward roles or activities that will enrich your work and reveal what gives you the greatest pleasure or fulfillment.

EXPERIMENT WITH SIDE PROJECTS

How can you discover what you're born to do, or even what you're good at? One approach is to use your free time to pursue interests or hobbies. A new weekend project can make you feel more energized throughout the week, whether you're learning how to play the piano or designing Lego robots with your kids.

Sometimes, a weekend project can inspire your coworkers, too. At a growing number of companies we've worked with, it's common to see a group of employees take up running together, start a book club, or share three-minute "how-to" talks at lunchtime about their current passion or hobby. At IDEO, weekend interests spill over into the workplace in the form of groups dedicated to activities like cycling and yoga. There are also frequent ad hoc knowledge-sharing sessions— everything from making Camembert (led by an engineer with a particular love for stinky cheese) to fabricating jewelry (taught by someone from our Toy Lab group who had studied jewelry design in Italy).

Side projects can be rewarding for their own sake. But they

> Take the time to ask yourself each day, "When was I at my best?"

may also lead to something that engages your creative energy at work. So search for ways your weekend projects might overlap with your working life. If your hobby is scrapbooking or video editing, for example, maybe you can apply those skills to delivering more compelling materials at work. Making that connection may take some creative thinking and effort, but if you're patient, an opportunity may present itself.

To identify new areas of interest and ability, experiment with lots of different activities—in your free time or at your job. The principles of prototyping can apply to trying new work roles as well: small, quick experiments provide the most bang for your buck. Get a taste of a different field or position before you make a drastic change and commit. Experiment with lots of different activities and see which ones resonate with you the most. Talk to your boss about exploring new responsibilities or help out a friend in another department. In these short-term roles, be mindful of the moments that you feel invigorated or at your best. Remember, this is about experimentation—don't be discouraged if you don't love the first thing you try. Reflect on what you liked about each activity and what you wished was different. Then make an informed choice about what to check out next. Once you start to think about your life and career as just another creative challenge, many different possibilities may come to light.

You may be surprised at the roles that attract you once you try them out. We know of lots of people who love jobs that others might find tedious or stressful: A manager in hospitality who deeply enjoys making others happy. A tax accountant who takes pride in deriving order out of chaos. An options trader who sees the stock market as an intricate, fascinating puzzle. They might never have discovered their hidden passion for those roles if they hadn't given them a try.

When seeking out new roles, don't be afraid to sign up for—or even propose—an interesting work-related project. You never know what it might grow into. And if higher-ups feel you lack proven experience in an area, demonstrate your abilities outside of work first. Having the personal energy and commitment to do everything you're expected to do at work *and* undertake an additional project out of passion makes a powerful statement. For example, Tom undertook his first book—*The Art of Innovation*—almost entirely on nights and weekends, just because he loved writing and wanted to capture some of the innovation stories and lessons we'd learned at the time.

It's not uncommon for the skills you develop on an individual work project to have broader applications. With a little luck—and a lot of perseverance—an interesting side project may even become your primary job over time. For example, Doug Dietz's initial work on GE's Adventure Series was a side project he was passionate about before it became his actual job responsibility.

In *The Ten Faces of Innovation,* Tom told the story of Ron Volpe, a supply chain manager at Kraft Foods Group. Ron launched a collaborative innovation project with a key client, Safeway, to find new ways to manage the complex flow of Kraft's products through Safeway's warehouses and stores. The project was just a small part of Ron's role at the time, and he thought of it as experimenting with a new mode of collaboration. But the project led to so many operational breakthroughs and garnered so much recognition from Safeway and the grocery industry that Ron spent the next phase of his career spreading innovation to Kraft teams all over the world. Ron soon became Kraft's customer vice president for supply chain innovation, seeking new ways to partner with diverse customers on six continents. He told us recently that this new role has sparked the most engaging, most interesting, and most rewarding work he's ever done. Ron says that applying creative confidence to his retailer relationships allows him and his customers to go beyond the day-to-day transactions and "focus on creating something bigger and more sustainable."

Ron didn't have to leave his company to experience a personal and professional transformation. It only took energy, optimism, and determination to turn his workplace experiment into a rewarding new role.

THE COURAGE TO LEAP

While everyone has enormous potential for creativity, our experience suggests that successfully applying creativity in your work and life requires something more: the courage to leap. All that potential energy will just fade away if you don't work up the nerve to unleash it, again and again.

To make that leap from inspiration to action, small successes are key. Just as fear of the first step holds us back at the beginning of a project, the weight of the status quo hinders us from making significant career changes. You may have entertained the thought "I could have been a writer," or "I wish I worked in health care," and stopped there. However, if you make the first step small enough, it can nudge you toward your goal. But you need to take that first step.

One corporate manager we know who started with small steps is Monica Jerez at 3M. We first met Monica a few years ago at an innovation conference in the Dominican Republic. For years, Monica had felt she was supposed to hide her creativity away in order to succeed in her career. But inspired by design thinking and empowered by a 3M growth-oriented leadership class, Monica became a whirlwind of action. As global portfolio manager in 3M's floor-care division, she read voraciously to find new sources of inspiration: books on innovation, business publications, and several daily newspapers. She visited the local Target store each week, walking every aisle in search of new ideas from product categories as far afield as beverages and oral care. She teamed up with a technical partner within 3M to help build a multidisciplinary team with design, technical, marketing, business, consumer insight, and manufacturing skills. She populated her office at 3M with so many products, prototypes, and Post-it notes that it looked like a design studio.

Originally, Monica had no budget for field research. But she didn't let that stop her. As the busy mom of four children, she had plenty of opportunity to study how families handle clutter. She had her house professionally cleaned and took a video of the cleaning in action, using the camera on her phone. The resulting video was so ripe with potential business opportunities that Monica commissioned more videos from 3M teams in twenty countries around the world. "My mind just became so big," Monica said with a laugh. "It redefined me."

Monica never considered herself to be the kind of creative person who would apply for a patent. But in the past year, she has filed for more than a dozen. A key innovation metric at 3M is the new product vitality index (NPVI), which tracks the percent of the company's sales that are from products introduced in the last five years. Monica's business unit's NPVI was *double* the company average last year. She was promoted to Hispanic Market Leader for 3M's Consumer & Office Business and has been recognized as a role model for other emerging leaders at the company. With newfound confidence in her creative contributions, she's having more fun at work, delivering more value for 3M, and inspiring others around her to do the same.

Monica's inspiration only turned into impact because she had the courage to start and the persistence to follow through. In our experience, one powerful way to commit to a new path is to just say it out loud to someone else. Tell a friend about the changes you plan to make in your life. Better yet, tell a group of people, who can give you constructive and continuous support.

MAKE A CHANGE

If you want to transform your life from mere duty to real passion, you have to start by realizing that your current situation is not the only option open to you. You can change how you live and how you work. Look at setbacks as the cost of trying new things. Don't be afraid to try and fail. The worst thing you can do is to play it safe, stick with the familiarity of the status quo, and not try at all.

Lauren Weinstein felt for some time that she didn't see eye to eye with the other law school students in her class. They were laser-focused on getting good grades and on learning all the legal precedents. At every turn, they seemed to ask, "What do previous cases suggest?" Lauren understood the importance of the rule of law but also found herself wondering about other matters. Who were the people in the case? What were their personal histories? Could that affect the outcome of a case? When she asked those kinds of questions aloud, she would get funny looks from her colleagues.

When she attended a class at the d.school for the first time, everything felt very foreign to her, but also very liberating. Instead of being pressured to recite back case law to get the "right" answer, she could experiment, and iterate toward a better solution. She didn't have to censor herself or be afraid of getting an answer "wrong." It was as if a weight had been lifted from her shoulders.

Before taking the class, Lauren had felt "a little creative," but she also knew herself to be timid and wishy-washy when it came to standing up for her ideas. Forced to come up with a hundred ideas in group ideation sessions—working on topics like innovative retirement options for baby boomers—she proved to herself she was creative, could handle uncertainty, and could initiate change in the world around her.

That confidence first blossomed in the classroom. But it eventually trickled back to the courtroom. At the same time Lauren was taking classes at the d.school, she was also preparing for a mock trial held at the Palo Alto Courthouse, to be argued before a judge and jury. The case concerned a construction worker who had been hit by a train. Lauren was assigned to argue the side of the victim. She knew the odds were against her: historically, the plaintiff's side in this particular trial had never won because the facts of the case favored the train company. In previous mock trails, the same details were presented in essentially the same way, and the outcome was always the same.

So Lauren came up with a new approach. When she shared her plan with her partner on the case, he tried to talk her out of it. But she was determined to try. During closing arguments, Lauren approached the jury box. She asked the jury members to close their eyes. "Imagine that you are having a nightmare. And in this nightmare, you are trapped on a train that is speeding down the tracks . . ." She had them picture the situation from the point of view of not only the people on the train but also the man who was hit. The case was no longer a straightforward recitation of facts and precedents; it was about what the construction worker experienced. The jury ultimately voted in her favor, and the judge said afterward that she had given the best argument he'd ever heard in that mock trial.

Asked how she got up the nerve to take a dramatically different approach, Lauren attributed it in part to the new creative confidence she had gained. "Nothing feels out of my comfort zone or the realm of possibility anymore," she says.

These possibilities are open to people of every age, in every job. Take Marcy Barton, a veteran fifth-grade teacher with four decades of experience in her field. Feeling helpless at the way she saw creativity draining out of kids, Marcy dove headfirst into a design thinking workshop at the d.school. She emerged ready to try something new to prepare the next generation of leaders for the twenty-first century.

Marcy restructured her entire curriculum from the ground up, reorganizing the state-required academic standards into design thinking challenges. In Marcy's next history class, kids didn't just sit quietly and read about the colonization of America; they flipped their desks over and climbed aboard the ships that would take them to the New World. They didn't just write math problems on the board; they used their mathematics skills to precisely calculate the size of the scale models they'd need to create a miniature American colony. Not only did the students show marked improvements in their standardized test scores, but more important, parents noticed that their kids asked better questions at home and began to engage more with the world around them.

Of course the opportunity to apply creative confidence is not limited to teachers. Salespeople, nurses, engineers—all can solve problems in new ways when they are not afraid to be creative.

If you are stuck in a "looks good, feels bad" position or job, think about the overlap between your personal passions and the workplace options that might be available to you. Learn new skills. Start writing the new story of your working life. Keep searching for and moving toward a role that will feel as good as it looks. When you reach it, you may realize that you have found your calling.

Start writing the new story of your working life.

CHAPTER 6

TEAM

CREATIVELY CONFIDENT GROUPS

While unlocking our own individual creative potential generates positive impact on the world, some changes require a collective effort. You need teamwork—the right combination of leadership and grassroots activism—to achieve innovation at scale. Change within organizations and institutions is seldom a solo activity. If you want your team to innovate routinely, you'll need to nurture a creative culture.

Take, for example, the cultural transition at Intuit shepherded by its vice president of design innovation, Kaaren Hanson. Back in the 1980s, Scott Cook had founded Intuit based on simplicity, beginning with its flagship Quicken product and expanding into now-familiar software programs like QuickBooks and Turbo-Tax. But eventually the company's growth slowed, and its executive leadership realized Intuit needed to go beyond incremental improvements to create breakthroughs. So Scott asked Kaaren—a young design director at the time—to help him reinvigorate the cycle of growth and innovation that had fueled the company's dramatic rise in its early days.

Looking for new tools, she took a course on customer-focused innovation at the d.school and learned about the principles described in this book. Kaaren also brought together ideas from such influential business thinkers as Geoffrey Moore, Fred Reichheld, and Clayton Christensen. The result was a way forward that the company called "Design for Delight"—referred to internally as D4D. For the employees at Intuit, design for delight means "evoking positive emotion by going beyond customer expectations in delivering ease and benefit so people buy more and tell others about the experience." Among the principles are: 1) deep customer empathy; 2) going broad to go narrow (i.e., seeking many ideas before converging on a solution); and 3) rapid experiments with customers.

Emerging from an executive offsite in 2007, D4D had the support of a lot of senior management. But Kaaren quickly learned that while buy-in from the top is necessary, it is not enough to guarantee success. The company got mired in what Kaaren calls "the talking phase," in which lots of people vocally express their support but no actual action is taken or progress made. "We made that mistake . . . twice," she says, referring to a second offsite over a year later. Key executives all agreed that Design for Delight was important to the future of the company and wanted to incorporate it in their groups. Yet D4D still remained more of a vision than a reality.

So in August of 2008, Kaaren recruited nine of the best design thinkers in the company to join her in a group called the Innovation Catalysts to spark creative initiatives and serve as coaches to help managers turn D4D ideas into action. The Catalysts came from design, research, and product management and were in positions close to the day-to-day operations of the company. Only two of them reported directly to Kaaren, but she gained access to about 10 percent of each of the other Catalysts' time (two days a month) and probably a much larger percentage of their mindshare. They went in search of opportunities to delight customers and spur innovative practices across the organization.

In one early project, a five-person Intuit team (including three Catalysts) created a user-friendly mobile app called SnapTax that helps customers prepare and file straightforward tax returns. The team observed dozens of young people from their target audience in places they would naturally frequent, like Starbucks and Chipotle. The Catalysts and their collaborators quickly went through eight rounds of software prototyping in the same number of weeks, gathering customer feedback and then iterating their design in each round to make the application stronger and easier to use.

To use the app, you simply take a photo of your annual W-2 Wage and Tax Statement and answer a few questions on your phone. Moments later, your tax forms are ready to ship. So how well does SnapTax fit with Intuit's definition of design for delight? Does it create positive emotion? Check. Does it go beyond customer expectations? Check. Does it create ease of use and a clear benefit to consumers? Check and check.

As Intuit began to design for delight among consumers, the company found itself renewing its culture of innovation. In other words, the creative process they used was contagious. As Kaaren says, "Fun is self-reinforcing. . . . Delighting customers grows our company and engages our employees."

The original group of Catalysts has grown to nearly two hundred, spread throughout the company, mentoring and collaborating with many hundreds more. Along with working on their own projects, they coach managers on the innovation process: facilitating brainstorms, helping conduct user interviews, building prototypes.

The Catalyst group is still being rolled out, but Intuit is already feeling its effects. Customer loyalty metrics like net promoter scores are up, as well as revenues, profits, and market capitalization. Roger Martin, dean of the Rotman School of Management at the University of Toronto, who has studied the company's performance in recent years, found Intuit now seizes new opportunities more quickly, and they've increased their mobile app offering from zero to eighteen within a span of two years. In 2011, Intuit appeared on *Forbes*'s annual list of the world's one hundred most innovative companies. Kaaren wants to "embed D4D into the DNA of Intuit by 2015," at which point the Catalysts won't even need to exist as a distinct group.

How did Kaaren and her colleagues build a creatively confident group, driven by new ideas? They got at least half a dozen things right:

- They gained broad executive support, which helped the Catalyst program cut across organizational lines.
- They launched grassroots action that required only modest middle-management commitment by using small percentages of employees' time.
- They leveraged one of the core principles of the company— simplicity—and gave it new life with the tangible concept of "Design for Delight."

- They handpicked the first few Catalysts to help jumpstart the program, knowing that it could be scaled up later, once the group had some momentum.

- They avoided big complex products owned by other departments and divisions within the company and instead launched small experiments in search of some early wins in new markets.

- They set a multiyear time horizon, recognizing that real culture change diffuses slowly through a large organization.

The Catalyst program has been a resounding success at Intuit. But it required a lot of experimentation, effort, and resilience every step of the way. Creatively confident organizations aren't built overnight. Even successful creative initiatives like the Catalyst program go through a series of phases before they "cross the chasm" and become part of the mainstream culture of an organization.

Mauro Porcini, chief design officer at PepsiCo, recently gave us his take on the phases that corporations go through to strengthen their ability to innovate.

We first met Mauro when he was head of Global Strategic Design at 3M, where he brought a bit of Milanese flair to Minnesota. After witnessing the evolution of innovation and design thinking for a decade at 3M, Mauro believes that companies progress through five phases as they gain creative confidence.

The first phase, Mauro says, is pure denial: executives and employees say, "We're not creative." It is an attitude that used to pervade traditional businesses, but that is changing. In the early days of IDEO, our clients were mostly interested in just the final outcomes of a project. Now, they work side by side with us, and nearly all of them are eager to see how we work so that they can learn how to embed creative confidence into their own culture.

Mauro calls the second phase "hidden rejection." This is where one executive strongly recommends and sponsors a new innovation methodology, and the other managers pay it lip service but then never actually commit to it. It's similar to the "talking phase" that Intuit went through. Plenty of times executive support does not translate into real progress. In other words, the organization falls into that familiar "knowing-doing gap," where words become a substitute for action.

Behavior change is hard, and lack of follow-through can occur for many reasons. Sometimes, it's because people aren't actually convinced that the new method will work, or they feel resistant to change. Perhaps they don't understand it well enough to implement the idea. Managers may start a project because their boss has asked them to, but then their focus fades away. Or as one employee told us, after his CEO encouraged the use of human-centered innovation, everyone knew to include a slide about a user in all their presentations to the CEO. They didn't actually see the value in speaking with end users; they were just trying to "check off a box" they knew was important to their CEO.

To get past the hidden rejection phase, frontline employees need to experience the principles of creative confidence for themselves. After they complete a design thinking cycle for the first time, they may begin to see how incorporating innovation methods into their own work could be helpful. The importance of direct experience mirrors psychology expert Albert Bandura's research on self-efficacy. Senior executives telling managers to boost innovation can have a limited effect. The most robust method to boost creative confidence is through guided mastery. Like learning how to drive a golf ball up the middle of the fairway, the most effective way of learning how to innovate routinely is through practice and coaching.

To build a creative organization, you need to build creative confidence among key players, one individual at a time. Innovation leader Claudia Kotchka helped introduce design thinking at Procter & Gamble. For her, getting people to experience the methodology firsthand was key. "I always say, 'Show, don't tell,'" Claudia explains. "The bottom line is, you just have to get as many people through it as you can. Because once someone experiences it, they are forever changed." Many clients have mentioned the importance of having trained innovation coaches within the company who can guide others toward creative confidence. While Intuit has its "Innovation Catalysts," other companies have their own versions, with names that range from "facilitators" to "co-conspirators."

> To build a creative organization, you need to build creative confidence among key players.

Mauro calls the third phase on the way to organizational creative confidence a "leap of faith." It occurs when someone in a position of power and influence recognizes the value in consumer-driven design thinking and puts his or her resources and support behind making a project happen. Dedicating space or resources to an initiative clearly signals that you want people to take risks and stretch their abilities, even if they fail.

Mauro calls the fourth phase the "quest for confidence." In this stage, an organization buys into innovation and searches for the best ways to leverage creative resources in support of the goals

TEAM

of the enterprise. Many clients we work with are in this phase, converting their initial innovation successes into methodologies they can use across the company.

The fifth phase is what Mauro calls "holistic awareness and integration." This is where innovation and constant iteration and designing with the customer experience in mind become part of a company's DNA. In this phase, teams routinely apply creative tools to the challenges they confront. It's creative confidence at an organizational level.

To start building a culture of innovation, you need support from both the top and the bottom—what Jeremy Utley at the d.school describes as "ground troops and air coverage." An initiative started from below is unlikely to survive if executives aren't on board. But a mandate from the top alone, as we've seen, won't incite passionate action either. People at every level need to understand how to influence culture and cultivate change.

In the rest of the chapter we'll talk about what an innovation culture and innovation leadership look like. Because leadership and culture are two closely intertwined factors that are essential to any creatively confident group.

KARAOKE CONFIDENCE IN YOUR WORK CULTURE

How do you make it safe to participate and engage in creative action? How do you gather the courage to try something new, knowing that you may be terrible at it initially? As toddlers, we were all bad at walking, but no one told us we should abandon the effort. As children, most of us had trouble mastering a bicycle, but we were encouraged to keep at it. As young adults, we discovered that driving a car wasn't as easy as we thought it would be—but we had a lot of motivation to improve our driving skills so that we could get a driver's license. So why is developing our creative confidence at work so fraught with peril? Why are we so prone to abandon a creative endeavor just because it's difficult early on?

Most people are reluctant to sing solo in public, but under the right conditions they willingly step up to the microphone. Tom first encountered karaoke machines in the smoky bars of urban Tokyo circa 1985, listening to drunken businessmen wailing off-key versions of Sinatra tunes. A first-time guest in the House of Karaoke might assume that the singer gains confidence solely through "liquid courage," since free-flowing alcohol seems almost an essential prerequisite for karaoke success. However, there are plenty of bars and restaurants where alcohol is available in great abundance but no one feels emboldened enough to belt out a tune. So we've since come to call the good-natured fun of a group songfest and the underlying cultural phenomenon "karaoke confidence."

Karaoke confidence, like creative confidence, depends on an absence of fear of failure and judgment. But it does *not* necessarily require native singing ability or immediate success. In fact, as any karaoke veteran can tell you, while the audience will notice—even comment on—singing talent, there is often as much appreciation and applause for a noisy but enthusiastic novice. Feeling the genuine support of the audience, that karaoke singer is encouraged to sing again, getting a bit better next time.

Karaoke confidence seems to rely on a few key ingredients. And we've noticed that those same ingredients are essential for encouraging cultures of innovation everywhere. Here are five guidelines that can improve your next karaoke experience—and your innovation culture:

- Keep your sense of humor
- Build on the energy of others
- Minimize hierarchy
- Value team camaraderie and trust
- Defer judgment—at least temporarily

Today, we apply these principles and mindsets across most of what we do. To foster creative confidence in a group setting, consider the social ecology of your team. Do people feel comfortable taking risks and experimenting with new ideas? Does the group encourage members to speak candidly, even when what they have to say may not be what everyone wants to hear? Do ideas flow up and down the hierarchy, or does the organization encourage people to "stick to official channels"?

At IDEO and the d.school, we seldom say, "That's a bad idea" or "That won't work" or "We've tried that before." When we disagree with someone else's idea, we push ourselves to ask, "What would make it better? What can I add to make it a great idea?" Or, "What new idea does that spur?" By doing so, we keep the creative momentum going instead of cutting off the flow of ideas. Throwing cold water on one person's contribution can bring the conversation to a halt; it is the back and forth of ideas that can lead you to new and unexpected places.

When a group embraces the concept of building on the ideas of others, it can unleash all sorts of creative energy. And the result looks something like this:

Four IDEO team members were driving back to their hotel after a long day in the field observing users. Suddenly they realized they were running low on Post-it notes. If you've seen a photo or video of our office, you know that Post-its are nearly essential tools for us to jot down interview observations, brainstorm ideas, record process steps, and so on. Nearly anything can go on a Post-it, which then gets placed on a wall or a board. Our entire office gets covered with them. So the team needed to quickly figure out how to get more Post-its at that late hour.

Somewhere in the space between punchy humor and cynicism, one team member wondered aloud if they should just recycle their used Post-its, holding up an old one when the same idea resurfaced. After the laughter subsided, that idea triggered a flood of additional suggestions. Everyone chimed in, riffing off previous ideas or inspired with new ones: a Post-it Rolodex, Post-it Bingo, Post-it maps. There are already something like four thousand unique Post-it products on the market. But as the group playfully tossed concepts back and forth, they invented a new one: a pad of Post-its interspersed with carbon paper. You write an idea on a Post-it, and when it goes up on the board you still have a carbon copy of it in the pad. Without any extra effort, the flow of ideas is memorialized on the pad itself. They immediately dubbed their new concept "Flowst-its" (rhymes with Post-its). The IDEO team member driving the car almost had to pull off the road, he was laughing so hard.

"Flowst-its" probably won't become a real product (though one designer started building a prototype). But the way it was generated exemplifies what creative collaboration looks like at its best. Exchanging ideas within a group of people who trust one another—without fear of judgment or failure—can feel electric. Your idea spurs another person's. The results might have been challenging for you to develop by yourself or probably would have taken longer. And coming up with them certainly wouldn't have been as much fun. In our experience working on thousands of innovation projects for many of the world's most demanding companies, the whole is much greater than the sum of the parts.

To make those kinds of innovation teams work, people have to buy into the mindset of working together toward a shared solution. No one person is responsible for the final outcome. It is the result of everyone's contribution. Instead of individuals protecting or promoting "my idea," colleagues become comfortable with group ownership. When a client recently asked the members of one of our project teams to write their names on each of their Post-its in an ideation session—as a way of assigning credit—we really struggled. We were so accustomed to fluidly building directly on each other's ideas in that setting, it felt really countercultural to say "This one is mine."

Collaboration works especially well when members bring different backgrounds or perspectives to the team. That's why we mix engineers, anthropologists, and business designers on project teams with surgeons, food scientists, and behavioral economists. By working in diverse multidisciplinary teams, we can get to a place that would have been impossible for one of us to reach alone. Bringing together a variety of life experiences and contrasting perspectives results in a creative tension that often leads to more innovative and interesting ideas.

RADICAL COLLABORATION AT THE D.SCHOOL

At the d.school, we often use team teaching as a way to spark multidisciplinary discussions and improve the classroom experience. In the traditional teaching approach, a professor delivers a lecture, probably the same one as last year and the year before that, while students try to write down every word. Maybe there's a bit of discussion afterward, but neither the students nor a teaching assistant are likely to offer any critique. Professors get in their cars and drive home, content in the belief that they've done their job well.

Once you blend professors from other departments and practitioners from the industry into the classroom, suddenly you create a group dynamic. When David first introduced the idea of team teaching at the d.school, professors imagined that they would all give mini-lectures, one after another, with maybe a little discussion at the end. What actually goes on is quite different: d.school professors challenge each other's ideas, sparking lively debates as they lean into the conflict. Multiple points of view get expressed. Instead of listening for the "right" answer from a professor alone at the dais, students have to think critically and ask questions to figure out where they stand. As members of the teaching team discuss ideas and challenge each other, both they and the students come up with new solutions and ways of thinking. It is a teaching model that gets students to exercise their own creative thinking. They experience firsthand that there are often several possible solutions in innovation.

Gathering diverse minds together can be particularly valuable when facing complex and multidimensional challenges. JetBlue Airways learned that lesson in the aftermath of a customer service nightmare in 2007. When an ice storm closed JFK International

Airport for six hours, weak links in the airline's operations led to flight disruptions that lasted six days. Some passengers were left stranded on the tarmac for ten hours at a time. The debacle cost JetBlue an estimated $30 million and prompted the airline's board to force out founder/CEO David Neeleman.

The root causes of JetBlue's slow recovery were subtle and multifaceted. To diagnose and solve the problem, the airline first brought in a consultant, spending more than a million dollars on lengthy reports. After no improvements resulted, Bonny Simi, then director of Airport and People Planning, proposed a different strategy to her boss. Instead of the top-down view, Bonny suggested they try a bottom-up approach with a multidisciplinary team. Her fresh outlook might stem partly from her eclectic and extraordinary background, which has included stints as an Olympic athlete (she raced down the luge track in Sarajevo, Calgary, and Albertville), a sportscaster, and a United Airlines pilot.

Bonny got the go-ahead for a single day's time from people representing every facet of frontline operations—pilots, flight attendants, dispatchers, crew schedulers, and others. Her plan was for them to map out together the complex interaction of events that gets triggered during "irregular operations," like inclement weather. There was a lot of doubt about the approach that first day. "Three quarters of the room were skeptics and the other quarter were cynics," says Bonny.

But they gave it a shot. They imagined a thunderstorm had canceled forty flights and then itemized every step of their recovery actions on yellow Post-it notes. Wherever a problem was identified, they wrote it on a pink Post-it. For example, they uncovered the fact that managers were using different formatting on a spreadsheet of flights to be canceled. The variations in how the data was presented led to miscommunication, confusion, and ultimately the cancellation of the wrong flights.

By the end of the day, there were more than a thousand pink Post-its, and Bonny got permission to form a task force to tackle the most important ones. Over the next several months Bonny worked with 120 JetBlue employees, mostly hourly workers who had volunteered. Empowered to change operations flow, people became "unbelievable evangelists" in supporting the effort, Bonny says.

By seeking answers from the collective, Bonny did more than she could ever have done alone. JetBlue reportedly began to recover from major disruptions 40 percent faster than before. "You realize that you aren't going to solve the problem sitting in an office," says Bonny. "You need to get out and talk to the people who are actually dealing with it, whether that's your customers or your frontline employees."

Multidisciplinary groups in any organization can cut through structural and hierarchical barriers to create an innovative mix of new ideas. The opportunities for such cross-pollination rise even further when you go beyond the boundaries of your company using open innovation. Instead of working only with internal resources, you describe a problem or quest on an open innovation site and let creative minds from all over the world help you solve it. You can develop your own open innovation platform to host the conversation or use third-party sites like InnoCentive.

After decades of relying on the creative capacity of IDEO and client teams alone, we founded OpenIDEO to build on the ideas of others on a much larger scale, using the power of an open innovation platform for social good. Since the digital community launched in 2010, it has attracted everyone from veteran designers to interested beginners representing a wide range of backgrounds and industries. Today, the community includes about forty-five thousand people from nearly every country in the world. They may never meet in person, but together they've already made a difference on dozens of initiatives—from helping revitalize cities in economic decline to prototyping ultrasound services for expectant mothers in Colombia.

CARE AND FEEDING OF AN INNOVATION TEAM

Working with people from diverse backgrounds is valuable, but that doesn't mean it's easy. It can lead to "creative abrasion." But as you work through conflicting opinions and points of view, new ideas can emerge.

To maximize the creativity of your team, keep in mind the principles that resident "d.shrink" Julian Gorodsky and former student Peter Rubin developed at the d.school to help team members be more supportive, honest, empathic, open, and comfortable enough with each other to encourage creative ideas.

1. **KNOW EACH OTHER'S STRENGTHS.** Imagine your team as a band of superheroes, each with his or her own special ability and weaknesses (or kryptonite). Divide the work to maximize team effectiveness and draw on each person's strengths.

2. **LEVERAGE DIVERSITY.** The dynamic tension between different viewpoints is what makes diverse teams a fertile ground for creativity. It can also be

---

a source of conflict and miscommunication. Teams that truly value diversity are willing to have the risky conversations rather than shy away from them.

3. GET PERSONAL. Leaving your personal life out of your professional life takes a toll on creative thought. Bring your whole self to work. Kick off team meetings by going around one by one with a "How are you doing, really?" check-in or a simple "Share something personal about yourself." Each person on your team brings unique life experiences to the table.

4. PUT THE "RELATIONSHIP" BACK IN "WORKING RELATIONSHIP." When we ask d.school teams what will matter most when they look back five years from now, the answer is usually "my relationship with my teammates," not just the project outcome. Keep things in perspective.

5. CRAFT YOUR TEAM EXPERIENCE IN ADVANCE. How will you help each other in the days ahead? What principles do you want to abide by? What do you hope to achieve—both personally and professionally—with the project?

6. HAVE FUN! Make it a priority to hang out and get to know each other. Having fun together will improve your collaboration. Go on a hike, get dinner, play a game, or work out as a team.

AN INNOVATION GREENHOUSE

When you deeply believe in creativity, you should weave it into the fabric of the company. Embed it into all your communications. Have it reflected in your hiring process and performance evaluations. Make it a part of your brand.

One overlooked opportunity to reinforce a culture of innovation is to build it into your physical space, into the work environments where your team spends the majority of its waking hours every workweek. An office environment can be numbing or it can be energizing. Teams—and especially team leaders—can look for opportunities to turn ordinary spaces into extraordinary ones. In *The Ten Faces of Innovation,* Tom described how the "Set Designer" optimizes the workplace to support creative energy; we are always looking for new ways to do so.

On a recent IDEO project, we worked with a classic American brand from the rock music world to develop a kind of collectible item that fans would hold on to for years. European designers Joerg Student and Elger Oberwelz sought inspiration from Airstream, makers of the aluminum trailer that traces its heritage back to the same designer who created Charles Lindbergh's *Spirit of St. Louis.* That sparked an idea: they could get a vintage Airstream trailer—a classic piece of Americana—to serve as their project space and help immerse them in the ethos of that era.

The team located a 1969 "Streamline Prince" Airstream and found a place on campus to park it. With classic pink flamingoes out front and vintage photos plastered on the walls, the trailer felt downright homey, though it was a bit cramped for the two designers (Elger is six foot three and Joerg is six foot five). But the drawbacks didn't limit the team's creativity. "Because of our special space," Joerg says, "we've never felt more inspired or had more fun on a project. It gave us so much energy and focus." You might not have room for (or need) a vintage Airstream trailer. But can you add or change something about your surroundings to make them a source of inspiration for your current project?

Another experiment in creative space we are trying out—on permanent loan from our friends at Steelcase—is something called the Digital Yurt. You can't miss the yurt when entering the lobby of our design studio in Palo Alto. Pure white, the Digital Yurt is a tapered cylinder about twelve feet in diameter that looks a bit like a small spaceship hovering just above the floor. It's a fun semiprivate meeting space for a small group, inspired by the picturesque tents used in Mongolia for centuries.

The Digital Yurt invites you to sit down and pick up a colored pencil.

The yurt has sparked countless informal business conversations. But our favorite source of cultural reinforcement comes not from the yurt itself but from the round white table that lives inside it. Remember when Mom taught you the rule about "No writing on the furniture?" It's one of a thousand rules we've internalized as part of being "well-behaved" members of modern society. But when you sit down in the yurt, you are given a clear signal that you've entered a space where you're encouraged to act differently. Almost everyone starts drawing on the circular white table inside the yurt, without even asking whether it's okay.

What triggers this reversal of "business as usual"? For starters, the table surface is made entirely of paper—doughnut-shaped white sheets stacked almost a foot high. Roughly the diameter of car tires, they can be torn off once they are filled with writing or artwork. Recessed in the center of that circular table is a large bowl filled with dozens of thick colored pencils. In other words, the environment in the yurt is sending you clear nonverbal signals. The paper provides the proverbial tabula rasa—a blank space waiting for you to customize it. And the well-worn pencils are clearly not there just for show. Often you will see the drawings of those who came before you, communicating instantly that here is a place where you can throw the old rules away and start drawing something new.

Space can affect us that way. Just as the right party atmosphere can bring out your "inner party animal," the right work environment can bring out your latent creative capacity. An open space facilitates communication and transparency. Wide stairways encourage serendipitous conversations among people from different departments. Ubiquitous writing surfaces prompt spontaneous ideation sessions. Dedicated project spaces can help the team be more cohesive.

So, be intentional about your workspace. For most organizations, space is their second-biggest expense—overshadowed only by the compensation of the people who work in that space. Companies should spend those space dollars wisely. If you want a team of smart, creative people to do extraordinary things, don't put them in a drab, ordinary space.

When the d.school was founded, we couldn't move into our permanent home right away. We had to relocate to four different places on campus four years in a row. The prospect was certainly daunting at the outset, but looking back, what we learned was invaluable.

The d.school started in a dilapidated, double-wide trailer on the outskirts of campus. The team tore down walls and then built new ones out of two-by-fours and clear polycarbonate. We formed tables out of doors on sawhorses. Students were free to do what they wanted, which included drilling into every surface they could see. From there, the school moved to an office space filled with rows and rows of computer terminals and cheap institutional carpet that we tore up to reveal the concrete floor below. Next, we relocated to a fluid dynamics laboratory lined with PhD offices around its perimeter. Our final home, where the d.school currently lives, used to be a drafting studio.

If you want a team of smart, creative people to do extraordinary things, don't put them in a drab, ordinary space.

Because the d.school had to move so often, it was forced to prototype its space again and again, to adapt it and test it with hundreds of students a year. After we lived in and used a space intensely for a while, a list of what worked and what didn't naturally emerged, informing the team's thinking when they designed the next space. While moving was difficult and stressful, it was also cathartic to start over and see things improve with every iteration.

TEAM

So the current d.school space embodies insights from all the previous versions.

Here are a few examples of the things we learned along the way (some of which are captured in a book called *Make Space* by Scott Doorley and Scott Witthoft, co-directors of the d.school Environments Collaborative):

- **KEEP PEOPLE TOGETHER BUT NOT TOO CLOSE.** We wanted close collaboration. But it was too crowded when we put all of the faculty at one table. Now each person has a desk, but they are clustered in an open space without divisions.

- **CONSIDER SOUND.** The trailer's wood and polycarbonate space dividers were meant to provide a feeling of openness and collaboration, but when we started using them, the importance of acoustic privacy became apparent. While the makeshift walls delineated different areas, they didn't stop sound, which made it hard to concentrate.

- **ADD FLEXIBILITY—IN THE RIGHT PLACES.** The team put everything on wheels: couches, tables, dividers, whiteboards, and supply carts. This flexibility allowed easy transition between varied uses. But it also proved there is a limit to flexibility, when it becomes more disorienting than liberating (like when the photocopier doesn't stay put).

- **TAILOR SPACES TO EXPERIENCES.** The staff also created a few "micro-environments" in the d.school. These closet-sized spaces, ranging from a "white room" for ideating to a plush lounge, suggest different modes of work and give teams a choice customized to their current activity.

- **CREATE AN ATMOSPHERE THAT GIVES PEOPLE PERMISSION TO EXPERIMENT.** At the d.school, most surfaces are raw plywood, foam, concrete, or whiteboard with minimal or no delicate finishes and no sense of preciousness. Rough materials signal "feel free to experiment," instead of "handle with care." This may seem like common sense, but it's not so common in the corporate world. Tom did a workshop years ago in a beautiful, brand-new corporate learning center for a well-respected Fortune 500 corporation. When he started to put up some posters to use in the workshop, someone stopped him, insisting that there was a rule about "no tape on the painted surfaces." When the surfaces in a learning center inhibit part of the learning process, it might be time to reassess.
- **DON'T BE AFRAID TO GO BIG WITH YOUR SPACE PROTOTYPES.** You can do full-scale prototyping on a shoestring. Chalk out the layout of a new space. Use twine or long runs of butcher paper to simulate walls. With cheap materials, you can start to visualize a new space in a way that helps the future occupants try out alternatives and visualize the "feel" of it.
- **USE DIPLOMACY.** Start with a small experiment before the big launch. Let people experience the low-fidelity full-scale prototype to get used to the idea. Bring people together to celebrate the transition to something new, whether it's christening a new building with a bottle of champagne or bestowing ceremonial keys on the group moving into a space.

Creating a self-imposed constraint like moving once a year may sound crazy, but it could also be just the push your group needs to constantly reinvent itself and stay on its toes. Look for opportunities to scramble things up. If you are planning a renovation, prototype ideas for the new space in your current one or at an interim location. If you have a new project, seize the opportunity to tailor your surroundings to that project. If changing your work environment becomes a regular occurrence, it will naturally become more reconfigurable and dynamic. So design your space for flexibility instead of inertia and the status quo.

USE LANGUAGE TO SHAPE YOUR CULTURE

Language is the crystallization of thought. But the words we choose do more than just reflect our thought patterns—they shape them. What we say—and how we say it—can deeply affect a company's culture. Anyone who has battled racism or sexism knows words *matter*. To change attitudes and behaviors, it helps to first change the vernacular. The same is true for innovation. When you influence the dialogue around new ideas, you will influence broader patterns of behavior. Negative or defeatist attitudes spawn negative or defeatist words. The opposite is also true.

Several years ago, we hosted a visit from Jim Wiltens, an outdoorsman, author, adventure traveler, and speaker who also teaches a program of his own design for gifted and talented children in Northern California schools. In his programs, Jim emphasizes the power of a positive vocabulary. And Jim leads by example. You will literally never hear Jim say, "I can't." He avoids saying those dreaded words by using more constructive versions

To change attitudes and behaviors, it helps to first change the vernacular.

that emphasize the possible, such as "I could if I . . ." He actually promises to pay his young students a hundred dollars if they ever catch him saying, "I can't."

Think Jim's approach sounds a bit simplistic for adults? Don't be too sure. When Cathie Black took over as president of Hearst Magazines, she noticed that negative speech patterns had created an environment hostile to new ideas. One person close to the company reported that the naysaying had become a cynical mantra for the executives. So Black told her senior team that every time they said, "we've tried that already" or "that will never work," she would fine them ten dollars. (Notice that the difference between business executives and teachers is that businesspeople levy the fine on *others*, not themselves.) The ten dollars was a trivial amount for them, but people don't like to be embarrassed in front of their colleagues.

After enforcing her rule just a few times, Black effectively wiped those expressions from the office vocabulary. Did the more positive vocabulary have a broader effect? During Black's tenure at Hearst, she kept flagship brands like *Cosmopolitan* healthy through one of the toughest periods in the publishing industry and launched new mega-successes like Oprah's *O* magazine. Meanwhile, Black also rose to become one of the most powerful women in American business.

Our version of the alternative to negative speech patterns is the phrase "How might we . . . ," introduced to us several years ago by Charles Warren, now salesforce.com's senior vice president of product design. "How might we . . . ?" is an optimistic way of seeking out new possibilities in the world. In a matter of weeks, the phrase went viral at IDEO and has stuck ever since. In three disarmingly simple words, it captures much of our perspective on creative groups. The "how" suggests that improvement is always possible—that the only question remaining is *how* we will find success. The word "might" temporarily lowers the bar a little. It allows us to consider wild or improbable ideas instead of self-editing from the very beginning, giving us more chance of a breakthrough. And the "we" establishes ownership of the challenge, making it clear that not only will it be a group effort, but it will be *our* group. Anyone who has worked with IDEO in the past decade or participated in OpenIDEO's social innovation challenges has undoubtedly heard that open-ended question.

But using this phrase is not just a matter of semantics. Thoughts become words, and words become deeds. If you get the language right, it affects behavior. Defenders of the status quo often say, "We've always done it this way" or "Nobody does it like that." With a series of "why?" questions, an eight-year-old could disarm such defenses. But adults sometimes forget the simple power of words. Try fine-tuning your group's vocabulary, and see the positive effect it has on your culture.

INNOVATION LEADERSHIP

The various ways of creating a culture of innovation that we've talked about so far are greatly influenced by the leaders at the top. Leaders can't dictate culture, but they can nurture it. They can generate the right conditions for creativity and innovation. Metaphorically, they can provide the heat and light and moisture and nutrients for a creative culture to blossom and grow. They can focus the best efforts of talented individuals to build innovative, successful groups.

In our work at IDEO, we have been lucky enough to meet frequently with CEOs and visionary leaders from both the private and public sectors. Each has his or her own unique style, of course, but the best all have an ability to identify and activate the capabilities of people on their teams. This trait goes far beyond mere charisma or even intelligence. Certain leaders have a knack for nurturing people around them in a way that enables them to be at their best.

One way to describe those leaders is to say they are "multipliers," a term we picked up from talking to author and executive advisor Liz Wiseman. Drawing on a background in organizational behavior and years of experience as a global human resources executive at Oracle Corporation, Liz interviewed more than 150 leaders on four continents to research her book *Multipliers: How the Best Leaders Make Everyone Smarter.* Liz observes that all leaders lie somewhere on a continuum between *diminishers,* who exercise tight control in a way that underutilizes their team's creative talents, and *multipliers,* who set challenging goals and then help employees achieve the kind of extraordinary results that they themselves may not have known they were capable of. At his best, Steve Jobs was a multiplier with his "reality distortion field." He convinced people around him that they could do the impossible and then magically enabled them to actually pull it off. And we can all probably remember at least one diminisher we've worked for, who made us feel that— no matter what we did—our efforts didn't really matter.

MULTIPLY THE IMPACT OF YOUR TEAM

Liz suggests that leaders who are multipliers can *double* the output of a team or company and improve morale in the process. Here's how you can become a multiplier:

- Be a "talent magnet" who attracts and retains the best, most creative people and helps them reach their highest potential.

- Find a worthy challenge or mission that motivates people to stretch their thinking.

- Encourage spirited debate that allows different views to be expressed and considered.

- Give team members ownership of results and invest in their success.

So use the strategies of a multiplier to help individuals in your group live up to their creative potential. And don't forget to be on the lookout for the creative leaders of tomorrow. If you do not yet have that mantle of authority in your organization, be a thought leader. Serve as a reverse mentor to others in the seat of power.

Warren Bennis, one of today's leading thinkers on the art of leadership, spent years studying groundbreaking groups such as the Walt Disney Studios (while Walt was still alive), Xerox PARC, and Lockheed's Skunk Works. Here are some of the highlights from his study of groups:

- Great groups believe they are on a mission from God. Beyond mere financial success, they genuinely believe they will make the world a better place.
- Great groups are more optimistic than realistic. They believe they can do what no one else has done before. "And the optimists, even when their good cheer is unwarranted, accomplish more," says Warren.
- Great groups *ship*. "They are places of action, not think tanks or retreat centers devoted solely to the generation of ideas." Warren characterized the successful collaborations he studied as "dreams with deadlines."

Part of the reason we can all understand the passion and performance of Warren's great groups is that most of us have been on one ourselves, whether undertaking a school project or tackling a new company initiative. Belonging to a strong creative team can be one of the most rewarding aspects of working life. And having experienced the heady feeling of being on a great team, we all long to be part of one again.

BRINGING INNOVATION TO P&G

Even with strong leadership, it is hard to achieve cultural change inside a large organization. To give you a better picture of how an organization can build creative confidence from the ground up, we'd like to share the story of how Procter & Gamble transformed itself during A.G. Lafley's first tenure as CEO. Among the strong leaders behind P&G's dramatic change, a central player was Claudia Kotchka, vice president for design innovation and strategy.

Called by some a "cultural alchemist," Claudia has just the

right mix of patience, perseverance, and force of personality to spread creative confidence across a huge corporation. Among her achievements at the largest consumer packaged goods company in the world was to—as *Fast Company* put it—"transform the company from a place that's good at selling 'more goop, better' into one whose products infuse delight into customers' lives." And she's proof positive that you don't need to have a degree in design to apply these methodologies. Before coming to P&G, she began her career as a certified public accountant.

When A.G. Lafley first became CEO, he asked Claudia to build design into the heart of the company. Most of Claudia's P&G career up until then involved marketing and general management, including running a successful service business inside the company, where she explored using design methodologies. Lafley told her that P&G was "just a technology company," but that technology alone wasn't enough. He wanted a total customer experience. She knew it would be hard to turn 100,000 employees into design thinkers inspired with creative confidence. When she read about design thinking for the first time, her reaction was "Whoa, this is so far from what we do. How am I going to get there? How am I going to learn this?"

But she was willing to try. She sent out a note to P&G business leaders and asked for their toughest problems, offering to help solve them. Her inbox was inundated. She then created an innovation fund to send a group of buttoned-down P&G executives to IDEO to work side by side with designers on some of those thorny problems.

It was a rough cultural transition: most of the P&G employees were immersing themselves in a design cycle that looked unlike anything they'd experienced before. Claudia remembers how a marketing executive called her in a panic from the design studio saying, "These people have no process! We have to teach them the P&G way." Claudia calmed her down and asked the exec to go with the flow a little longer. And she did, becoming a fervent supporter of the new innovation methods.

Claudia later brought in innovation practitioners to conduct workshops at P&G. Eventually employees were trained as facilitators of the process so they could lead the workshops themselves. In one workshop, the Olay team wrestled with the problem that consumers had trouble distinguishing the different products in the Olay line. The team had planned to redesign the packaging. But they scrapped that solution after they realized through the workshop that by the time the consumer got to the store shelves, it was too late—if they didn't already know what they were looking for, they weren't going to figure it out in the store. So the team instead reframed the question, which guided them toward building a website called "Olay for You." It helped consumers figure out what product they should use and gave them personalized recommendations before they went to the store.

P&G developed a steady stream of products that way. But what was far more important to Claudia was the creative confidence P&G executives gained from going through the design cycle.

What did the workshops look like? In a whirlwind three days, employees were guided through applying the process of brainstorming, researching end users, building prototypes, and fleshing out concepts to a problem they were struggling with. High-level executives often arrived at these workshops expecting to start with a PowerPoint presentation. "And step one, we throw them in with consumers. They are freaking out. They want to see an agenda, and we're like, nope, sorry," says Claudia. "The workshop moves so fast they don't have time to question the process. They are immediately engaged." One of P&G's vice chairs told Claudia it was the best training he had ever had, both because it didn't *feel* like training and because he was solving a real problem that was important to his group. "Every single one of those workshops was a hit because they would come away with insights they never expected," says Claudia. A.G. Lafley even came to Claudia with a problem—how can we get the business units to work together instead of being siloed in their own profit centers?

With permission to experiment, Claudia and P&G figured out a number of things during this time of organizational change:

- **TESTIMONIALS—NOT JUST METRICS AND RESULTS— ARE PERSUASIVE.** Stories and votes of confidence from those who had experienced the new innovation methodology were key in convincing others of its value. "People had to believe that the workshops were worth their time or they wouldn't do them," Claudia says.
- **PROTOTYPING IS BOTH A POWERFUL INNOVATION TOOL AND A POWERFUL CULTURAL VALUE.** "Everything is a prototype," says Claudia. "So, we would do an org change and I would say to everyone, 'It's a prototype.' Which means (a) I have permission to be wrong and (b) I want your feedback if it's not working." Ideas were no longer sacred. If your idea was dismissed, you didn't feel bad or feel as if your idea had gotten killed. "That's magic. It's so huge. Because when people get locked into something, it's hard to get them off of it, and then their feelings are hurt," says Claudia.

- **TRAINING ALL THE DISCIPLINES HELPS DISSEMINATE CHANGE.** Training people from *all* disciplines helped instill creative confidence organization-wide: purchasing, supply chain, market research, marketing, R&D—even finance. "Finance people are amazingly creative," says Claudia. "The workshops were the first time they talked to consumers, and they loved it. And you know what they would say? I'm bringing my whole self to the job." As a result, there were facilitators throughout the organization: "HR would be sitting around saying, 'What are we going to do about the retention of women?'" says Claudia. "And the facilitator would say, 'I can help us fix that.'"

Claudia helped bring creative confidence to P&G by getting as many people as possible to experience small successes for themselves. Today, P&G has three hundred facilitators throughout the company who continue to train employees in how to embed innovation thinking in every aspect of the organization.

As A.G. said of Claudia upon her retirement from P&G, "Under Claudia's leadership, in only seven years, we've built world-class design capability at P&G. She has helped integrate design and design thinking into how we innovate and how we operate as a company. Her passion for the power of design has strengthened our brands and our business."

TAPPING THE CREATIVITY IN US ALL

In a world filled with so much creative potential, it is dangerous to assume that all the good ideas are found at the top. Yet we've seen that attitude expressed in more than one global corporation: the C-level executives map out their master plans, and the rest of the organization is left to implement them. If your CEO has enough good ideas to fuel the company's growth objectives in perpetuity, maybe you don't need to tap into the reservoir of talent at other levels of the organization. But the most innovative companies in the twenty-first century have transitioned from command-and-control organizations to a participatory approach that involves collaboration and teamwork.

In a world filled with so much creative potential, it is dangerous to assume that all the good ideas are found at the top.

They draw on the whole brain of the company, gathering the best ideas and insights wherever they find them. They are open to listening to people from the front lines of their operation. They nurture the innovative spirit in all their team members so that ideas percolate up through the organization.

Frank Gehry is one of the greatest living architects, famous for designing iconic buildings like the Guggenheim Museum in Bilbao, Spain, with its dramatic sheathing of wavy titanium. Early in his career, he had a job washing airplanes in a small airport in Southern California. Frank says he liked that simple job, and if someone had just taught him to fly he might have stayed there. Imagine that. The manager of that little aviation company had one of the most creative architects of the past hundred years washing planes for him. But neither the manager nor his employee knew how much potential energy stood out on the tarmac, just waiting to be unleashed.

Is there a creative genius doing spreadsheets in your accounting department? Is there a future Fortune 500 CEO in your sales team? Is there an employee just waiting for the right opportunity or partner to unlock billions of dollars of value for your organization? Why not set up a process or system of participation that allows those budding innovators to express their ideas? Why not give people on your team or organization more creative license, more of a chance to reach their full potential? When you find the innovator inside your team members, the whole company can benefit. Give people a chance to build their skills. You might discover someone you hadn't noticed before who is poised for greatness. Toyota stays among the top automotive companies in the world by empowering every single employee to propose innovations as an intrinsic part of his or her job. The most creative companies we know have built a structure for encouraging creative energy at every level of the company.

To grow the creative confidence of your organization, create a culture of innovation. Draw on the power of multidisciplinary teams, encourage those around you to build on the ideas of others, and lead in a way that multiplies the capabilities of everyone in your organization. As d.school executive director George Kembel sometimes describes it, one way to spur more innovation is to nurture the innovators.

CHAPTER 7

$M \, o \, V_E$

CREATIVE CONFIDENCE TO GO

In Chapter 4, we talked about the importance of action. And if we were with you in person at a workshop, we'd already be out in the field observing unmet human needs, prototyping a new idea, collecting stories, or at least rearranging the room to suit our purposes. So why not set this book aside right this minute and run out to try putting one of your favorite ideas into action? Go ahead. We'll wait right here . . .

How did that go? We know that getting started is hard. But unleashing our inner creativity is like so many things we try; the more we practice, the easier it gets. The tools in this chapter are intended to help you practice unlocking your creative thinking as a bridge to creative confidence.

Each exercise corresponds with an innovation question or

challenge. Don't feel compelled to try them all. If a particular topic doesn't resonate with the concerns you are facing today, then chances are the tool won't either.

We'll begin with a couple of exercises you can start doing by yourself right now. Others you can use the next time you are in a group or team setting. Try a few of them out. See if they help you flex your creative muscles.

Some of these techniques will seem incredibly simple. That's good since it means there's a low barrier to entry. We hope that you will attempt at least one idea (and share it with your colleagues, if appropriate). The value lies not in the idea, however, but in the *action*.

CREATIVITY CHALLENGE #1:

PUSH YOURSELF TO THINK DIVERGENTLY AND CREATIVELY.

Actively engaging in exercises that foster divergent or unconventional thinking can encourage the generation of ideas. When you are searching for innovative solutions on your own, mindmaps can be a powerful way to come up with ideas or to gain clarity about a topic of exploration. They are extremely versatile, and we use them all the time. From coming up with ideas for a family vacation to identifying home projects to tackle over the weekend, mindmaps can be used for all sorts of problem solving. They help you chart the recesses of your mind surrounding one central idea. The further you get from the center of the map, the more hidden ideas you can uncover.

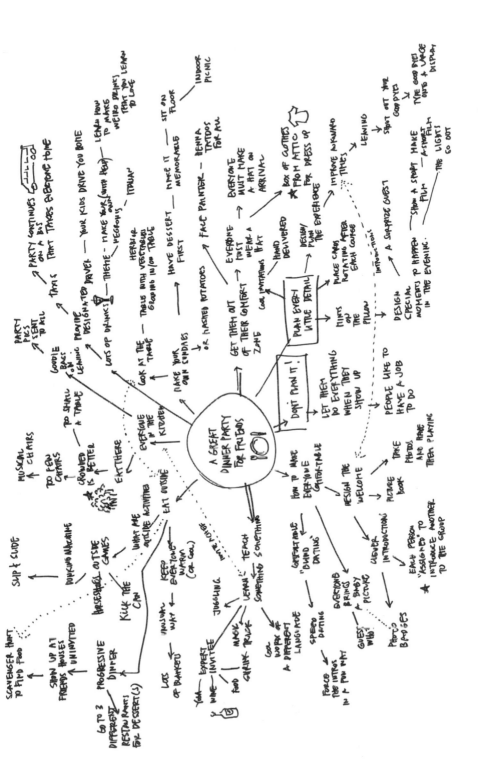

A GREAT DINNER PARTY FOR FRIENDS

- DON'T PLAN IT!
  - LET THEM DO EVERYTHING WHEN THEY SHOW UP
  - PEOPLE LIKE TO HAVE A JOB TO DO

- GET THEM OUT OF THEIR COMFORT ZONE
  - EVERYONE MUST WEAR A HAT
  - EVERYONE MUST MAKE A HAT ON ARRIVAL
  - FACE PAINTER
  - HENNA TATTOOS FOR ALL
  - BOX OF CLOTHES FROM ATTIC FOR DRESS UP
  - IMPROVE AWKWARD TIMES
    - LEANING

- PLAN EVERY LITTLE DETAIL
  - COOL INVITATIONS
    - HAND DELIVERED
    - DESIGN/PLAN THE ENTIRE BAG
  - PLACE CARDS ROTATING AFTER EACH COURSE
  - MINTS ON THE PILLOW
  - DESIGN SPECIAL MOMENTS TO HAPPEN IN THE EVENING
  - A SURPRISE GUEST
  - INTRODUCTIONS
  - SHOW A SHORT FILM
    - MAKE A SHORT FILM
  - TYPE GOOD BYE!
    - THE LIGHT GO OUT
    - SHOUT OUT YOUR GOOD BYES
  - LEANING

- HAVE DESSERT FIRST
  - MAKE IT MEMORABLE
  - SIT ON FLOOR
  - INDOOR PICNIC
  - LEARN HOW TO MAKE WEIRD DRINKS (WITH HEAT) / MERINGUES
  - "ITALIAN"
  - THEME – MAKE YOUR OWN DESSERT
  - MAKE YOUR OWN SUNDAES
  - LOOK AT THE TABLE
  - OR MASHED POTATOES

- EAT OUTSIDE
  - EVERYONE IN THE KITCHEN
  - EAT THERE
  - CROWDED IS BETTER
  - TOO FEW CHAIRS
  - MUSICAL CHAIRS
  - TOO SMALL A TABLE
  - GOODIE BAGS
  - LEAVING PRESENT
  - PARTY PIES SENT TO ALL
  - PARTY CONTINUES ON A BUS
  - TAXIS
  - YOUR KIDS DRIVE YOU HOME
  - PART TAKES EVERYONE HOME
  - DESIGNATED DRIVER
  - LOTS OF DRINKS
  - TABLES WITH VEGETABLES GROWING IN/ON TABLE
  - HERBS ETC

- WHAT ARE THE OUTLINE ACTIVITIES
  - KEEP EVERYONE WARM (OR COOL)
  - NAPKINS MACHINE
  - KICK THE CAN
  - INTO THE NOISE
  - LOTS OF BLANKETS
  - JUGGLING
  - UNUSUAL WAY
  - MAGIC TRICK
  - CRANK TRICK
  - SLIP & SLIDE
  - SCAVENGER HUNT TO FIND FOOD
  - SIGN UP AT FRIENDS' HOUSES UNINVITED
  - GO TO 3 DIFFERENT RESTAURANTS FOR DESSERT(S)
  - PROGRESSIVE DINNER

- LEARN/TEACH SOMETHING SOMETHING
  - EXPERT INVITEE
  - FOOD
  - WINE
  - GO WORK IN A DIFFERENT LANGUAGE
  - SPEED DATING
  - COMFORTABLE "BLIND DATING"

- HOW TO MAKE EVERYONE COMFORTABLE
  - DESIGN THE WELCOME
  - PICTURE BOOK
  - TAKE PHOTOS AND HAVE THEM PLAYING
  - CLEVER INTRODUCTIONS
  - EACH PERSON "ASSIGNED" TO INTRODUCE ANOTHER TO THE GROUP
  - EVERYONE BRINGS A BABY PICTURE
  - GUESS WHO?
  - PHOTO BADGES
  - FORCE THE INTROS IN A FUN WAY

TOOL: Mindmaps

PARTICIPANTS: This is usually a solo activity

TIME: 15–60 minutes

SUPPLIES: Paper (the bigger the better) and pen

INSTRUCTIONS

1. On a large blank piece of paper, write your central topic or challenge in the middle of the paper and circle it. For example, you might write "A great dinner party for friends."

2. Make some connections to that main topic and write them down, branching out from the center as you go. Ask yourself, "What else can I add to the map that is related to this theme?" In the dinner party example, you might write down "everyone in the kitchen" and "make your own sundaes" as two avenues of thought. If you think one of your ideas will lead to a whole new cluster, draw a quick rectangle or oval around it to emphasize that it's a hub.

3. Use each connection to spur new ideas. For example, under "make your own sundaes," you might write "have dessert first" or "cook at the table."

4. Keep going. You are done when the page fills or the ideas dwindle. If you are feeling warmed up but not finished, try to reframe the central topic and do another mindmap to get a fresh perspective. If you feel you've done enough, think about which ideas you would like to move forward with. After drawing the mindmap shown here, David threw a big dinner party in which guests changed tables after each course, enabling them to talk to everyone in the room. Each challenge presents an opportunity for innovation.

Generally the first set of ideas that branch from the center will feel clichéd or obvious. That happens to everyone. Those concepts already were in your head and were just waiting to be captured on paper. As the map progresses, however, your mind will open up, and you'll likely discover some wild, unpredictable, dissociative ideas.

As you experiment with mindmapping, you may find it valuable in all sorts of creative endeavors. As David's former colleague Rolf Faste used to say, mindmapping can:

1. Get you started and help you overcome your fear of the blank page.
2. Help you look for patterns.
3. Reveal the structure of a subject.
4. Map your thought process and record the evolution of an idea. (You can trace it backwards later in search of new insights.)
5. Communicate both the ideas and the process to others, so that you can guide them on the same mental journey.

You may be wondering when a mindmap is better than an ordinary list. Lists are great at keeping track of things we don't want to forget. But the to-do list assumes we know what to put on it, whereas, at the start of a mindmap, we don't yet know where it's going to lead us. Mindmaps are good at facilitating divergent or unconventional thinking; lists are good for capturing the best answers among the thoughts you already have. Mindmaps help to *generate* ideas. As such, mindmaps are particularly useful early in the creative process. Lists are better later on, when you want to capture the ideas you've generated and are looking for the best solution to pursue. Each of the chapters in this book started as a mindmap. Later they evolved into lists of stories and ideas that we wanted to weave together. When you are trying to create something new, use mindmaps to generate ideas and lists to capture the best ones. Together, they can be a powerful combination.

CREATIVITY CHALLENGE #2:

INCREASE YOUR CREATIVE OUTPUT.

Anyone who studies dreams will tell you that if you want to remember your dreams, you need a dream journal *right beside the bed*. The moment you wake up—whether it's the middle of the night or in the morning—you should capture those dreams before they fade away. The same holds true with your waking "dreams," your partially or fully formed ideas, your glimpses of possible futures. If you want to maximize your creative output, don't rely on short-term memory.

Even if you never get to experience Andy Warhol's fifteen minutes of fame, you're likely to have your own moments of brilliance once in a while. When that happens, make an effort to capture your ideas right away because your short-term memory holds a thought for only fifteen to thirty seconds. One simple way to have more ideas in your arsenal is to start keeping track of them as they occur.

TOOL: Fifteen Seconds of Brilliance

PARTICIPANTS: This is a solo activity

TIME: 10 minutes per day

SUPPLIES: Paper and pen, or a digital means of keeping notes

INSTRUCTIONS

When you have an idea or observe something intriguing, take note of it. The actual means of capturing the idea doesn't matter as much as having it with you at all times. Choose a method or a technology that fits with your lifestyle and your personality:

- Digital tools are great, but paper still works exceptionally well. Tom always has a pen and a simple folded piece of paper in his back pocket. He also keeps a small pad of paper on his bedside table with a lighted pen that he can use to jot down an idea while reading or in the middle of the night without fear of waking up his wife.
- As we mentioned earlier, David has a whiteboard marker in his shower, so he can write down a passing idea before it disappears.
- IDEO partner Brendan Boyle has experimented with various forms of "idea wallets" designed specifically to record his thoughts.
- On the iPhone, Siri will let you dictate a quick mental note. An increasing number of options also exist on other platforms.
- Your laptop or tablet has all kinds of notepad applications. But we think you'll get more functionality out of purpose-built programs like Evernote, specifically designed to store such ideas.

So increase your odds in the war against lost ideas. You'll be amazed at how many good ideas you end up with when you make an effort to jot down those sudden moments of insight. Our brains are constantly making connections and associations with people, things, and ideas we come in contact with. Don't let those serendipitous insights go to waste.

Here's one quick, simple exercise to get your creative muscles warmed up. We learned it from David's mentor, Bob McKim, back when David was a product design student. It's called Thirty Circles, and you can do it on your own or in a group. The goal is to push people to test their creativity by turning circles into recognizable objects in a very short period of time.

TOOL: Thirty Circles Exercise

PARTICIPANTS: Solo or groups of any size

TIME: 3 minutes, plus discussion

SUPPLIES: Pen and a piece of paper (per person) with thirty blank circles on it of approximately the same size. (We usually preprint identical circles on an oversized sheet of paper, but you can also just ask everyone to draw their own thirty circles on a blank piece of paper.)

INSTRUCTIONS

1. Give each participant one Thirty Circles sheet of paper and something to draw with.
2. Ask them to turn as many of the blank circles as possible into recognizable objects in three minutes (think clock faces, billiard balls, etc.).

3. Compare results. Look for the quantity or fluency of ideas. Ask how many people filled in ten, fifteen, twenty, or more circles? (Typically most people don't finish.) Next, look for diversity or flexibility in ideas. See if the ideas are derivative (a basketball, a baseball, a volleyball) or distinct (a planet, a cookie, a happy face). Did anyone "break the rules" and combine circles (a snowman or a traffic light)? Were the rules explicit, or just assumed?

TIPS FROM THE FIELD

Besides being a great warm-up exercise, Thirty Circles offers a quick lesson about ideation. When you generate ideas, you are balancing two goals: fluency (the speed and quantity of ideas) and flexibility (ideas that are truly different and distinct). We know from experience that it's easier to have a great idea if you have many to choose from. But if you have a lot of ideas that are just variations on a theme, you might really have only one idea with twenty-nine other versions. When you combine fluency and flexibility, you can generate a rich array of concepts to choose from.

LEARN FROM OBSERVING HUMAN BEHAVIOR.

A fundamental principle of innovation or creative thinking is to start with empathy. On the path from blank page to insight, sometimes people need a tool to help with what comes *next*: synthesis. You've gone into the field in search of knowledge, meeting people on their home turf, watching and listening intently. But synthesizing all that data can be a little daunting.

Take control of your field observations by organizing them with an "empathy map"—a tool inspired by IDEO and further developed at the d.school.

TOOL: Empathy Maps

PARTICIPANTS: Solo or groups of two to eight people

TIME: 30–90 minutes

SUPPLIES: Whiteboard or large flip chart, Post-its, and pens

INSTRUCTIONS

1. On a whiteboard or a large flip chart, draw a four-quadrant map (see diagram). Label the sections with "say," "do," "think," and "feel," respectively.

2. Populate the left-hand quadrants with Post-its that capture each of your individual observations, using one Post-it per idea. Place observations about what people DO in the lower-left quadrant, and place observations of what people SAY in the upper-left quadrant. Try color-coding your observations, using green Post-its for positive things, yellow Post-its for neutral, and pink or red for frustrations, confusion, or pain points. The key is not to record everything, but instead to capture what stands out.

3. When you run out of observations (or room) on the left side, begin to fill the right side with Post-its, inferring what people THINK in the upper-right quadrant and what they FEEL in the lower-right quadrant. Pay attention to people's body language, tone, and choice of words.

4. Take a step back and look at the map as a whole. Try to draw some insights or conclusions from what you have just written down, shared, and talked about. These questions serve as a good prompt for a discussion of insights. What seems new or surprising? Are there contradictions or disconnects within or between quadrants? What unexpected patterns appear? What, if any, latent human needs emerge?

TIPS FROM THE FIELD

The key to extracting value from observing human behavior is to come away with real insights. This can be challenging, but the exercise is worth the time and effort. As you build up confidence, ask yourself, "Is this a real insight?" Our advice is to look for takeaways that help you see your topic or subject from a new perspective. Try to come up with several that feel novel. As you spend more time with others exploring your topic or subject, patterns will emerge. Some insights will prove to be more pivotal than others.

ENCOURAGE AND ACCEPT CONSTRUCTIVE FEEDBACK.

To practice creative confidence on a team, members need to feel free to experiment, even during early efforts when results will be far from perfect. For that experimentation to translate into learning, however, at some point you need feedback, in order to identify weaknesses and make adjustments the next time. We all instinctively know that constructive critique is essential. And yet it can be hard to listen to and absorb feedback without letting our egos and defensiveness distract us from what may be a valuable message.

We have found the tool "I like/I wish" immensely useful in introducing constructive critique into the innovation process. I like/I wish is helpful anytime feedback is needed. This framework can be used in a small group to review concepts or in a large group to receive feedback about a class or workshop experience. Feedback starts with honest praise, in the form of positive sentences that begin with the phrase "I like . . ." Suggestions for improvement then begin with "I wish . . ."

TOOL: I Like/I Wish

PARTICIPANTS: Groups of any size

TIME: 10–30 minutes

SUPPLIES: A means of recording feedback. For example, in a large group we frequently keep a Word document open and type up notes in real time. In a smaller setting, Post-its or index cards will work.

INSTRUCTIONS

1. Set the tone for a constructive conversation and explain the "I like/I wish" method. For example, you could say, "I am

interested in hearing about how this workshop experience has been for you. Please express feedback in the form of I like/I wish. You might say, 'I like that we have started on time every morning. I wish we had 30 minutes every afternoon to stretch our legs.'" We have found it helpful to model good feedback by demonstrating "I like/I wish" in action.

2. The participants take turns, sharing I like/I wish statements, while the facilitator records their statements. For example, if you are reviewing work in progress for a new personal finance software tool, you might offer support such as "I like that you have incorporated five different ways for customers to view their current financial status." After describing other pluses, you might then say something like "I wish we could make the website easier for first-time users to navigate" or "I wish we could help people examine their financial situation from the long-term perspective of years, not the short-term perspective of months." Make sure people receiving feedback just listen. This is not a time to defend decisions or challenge the critique. Ask everyone to listen and accept it as a well-meaning offer of help. You can ask for clarification and engage in further discussion at a later time.

3. Stop when participants run out of things to say in both the "I like" and "I wish" categories.

You may want to gather just the "I like" comments first and then ask for the "I wish" statements. In other groups, it may make sense to let the give-and-take of statements flow organically. Feel free to play with the format.

"I like/I wish" signals that what you are stating is your opinion—it's not an absolute. Instead of pointing fingers, you are offering your view or perspective. The goal is to move the listener away from a defensive posture so that he or she can more objectively consider alternative ideas and take them to heart, when appropriate. We all tend naturally to become invested in our own ideas and seek to defend them. But in a creative culture, candid feedback that is sensitively conveyed is a sign that colleagues care enough to speak up. The message can be delivered quite clearly, without resorting to the negative language of "That will never work" or "We tried that before and it failed."

CREATIVITY CHALLENGE #6:

WARM UP A GROUP.

Creativity thrives amidst free-flowing social discourse. To get a roomful of strangers to innovate, you may want to begin by breaking down some social barriers. When this exercise is done right, the room will be abuzz with chatter and laughter, and participants will be more open to what comes next.

TOOL: Speed Dating
PARTICIPANTS: Pairs in groups of any size
TIME: 15–20 minutes total, 3 minutes per round
SUPPLIES: Paper printed with a set of questions for each participant. Several different sets of questions will be needed to accommodate the entire group.

INSTRUCTIONS

1. Give each person a list of open-ended questions. Several different sets of questions should be spread throughout tables in the room so that people aren't continually being asked the same questions.

    Examples of possible questions:

    How would your closest family members describe you?

    If you had a million euros to spend in a way that benefits humanity, what would you do?

    What do you wish your parents had told you?

    What was a live performance or show you really loved, and why?

2. Ask each person in the room to pair up with someone they don't know very well or have never met. This may involve getting up and moving seats.
3. Have one person in each pair ask a question from the list. Allow three minutes for the other person to answer.
4. Have each pair switch roles and repeat, asking a different question on the list.
5. Tell everyone to find a new partner and repeat the process for a couple more rounds.

TIPS FROM THE FIELD

You want to keep people moving to create a well-orchestrated round-robin. Be proactive about timekeeping. Assign someone to be a facilitator or timekeeper. To add a little fun, use a buzzer or gong to announce that time is up.

Depending on the nature of the working session that will follow the Speed Dating exercise, you can tailor some of the open-ended questions to be inspirational and loosely related to your topic. For example, if the objective of the meeting is to discuss the future workspace of the organization, one of the prompts may be "Describe an inspiring space you have worked in."

Give a little thought to the types of questions you use. Meaning-of-life questions and superlative questions (the most, the best, the worst) can cause people to stall out or draw a blank. The whole purpose is interaction. So if your question stumps your partner for even a handful of seconds, it's not quite right. Try the questions out on someone before you use them in a group setting.

If your group is uncomfortable with an activity that includes the word "dating" in the title, call it Speed Meeting—which we have found works with Nobel laureates.

CREATIVITY CHALLENGE #7:

ELIMINATE HIERARCHY TO IMPROVE IDEA FLOW.

While Speed Dating is useful in situations where people don't know each other well, sometimes in group meetings you will encounter the opposite problem: a group where people know each other *too* well. Or, more specifically, a group in which hierarchy is so well established that the more junior members in the room self-edit and defer to the executives rather than putting their best ideas on the table.

To reduce hierarchy (which inhibits conversation) and self-censoring (which is equally limiting), the d.school has recently been experimenting with a "nickname warm-up." Using a stack of colorful names the instructors have prepared in advance, the activity is a way to temporarily level out the organization during a creative working session. Each participant is given a persona to allow them to "try on" new behaviors.

TOOL: Nickname Warm-up

PARTICIPANTS: Groups of six to twelve people per facilitator

TIME: A few minutes per person

SUPPLIES: Name tags for all participants with the fake names written out. A hat and a ball for each facilitator.

INSTRUCTIONS

1. Each participant reaches into the hat, draws out a name tag, and puts it on. Use names that lend themselves to humor and emotion. Teams tend to produce their best work when the group is having fun. Some of the monikers can imply a big dose of street credibility, while others suggest quirky

personalities—for example, Dr. Fabulous, Squirt, Mr. Big Heart, The Clumsy Entertainer, or The Rooster.

2. The facilitator gathers the group in a circle and tosses the ball. Whoever catches it introduces themselves using their new nickname and then tells a short story (created on the spot) about how they acquired this nickname as a child.

3. After their self-introduction, they toss the ball to a new person, until everyone has had a chance to share their new name and story.

4. The rule for the rest of the workshop—strictly enforced—is that everyone must use only these nicknames when referring to themselves or others.

TIPS FROM THE FIELD

Do the name tags work? Although this is a relatively new exercise, experience so far suggests that the answer is yes. At a recent management event, the CEO of a global hospitality company drew the "Squirt" nickname. There was a pregnant pause in the room as everyone waited to see how he would react. But he gamely played along through the rest of the workshop, and the organizers felt it contributed to an open environment in which people could speak freely.

The goal is to flatten out the hierarchy, so it's important to get the senior people in the room to participate. Leading by example will naturally break some of the barriers to free-flowing collaboration.

CREATIVITY CHALLENGE #8:

EMPATHIZE WITH CUSTOMERS, EMPLOYEES, AND OTHER END USERS.

One way to develop more empathy with—and gain new insights about—your customers is to look beyond the narrow definition of your offering and consider the customer's total experience. The more broadly you define the customer experience, the more opportunities you can identify for improvement.

Say, for example, you make interior house paint. You could focus narrowly on the characteristics of the product itself, on making the paint less drippy or making it cover a surface in a single coat. But you'll find many more opportunities for innovation if you think about the arc of the customer experience. In something as simple as repainting a bedroom, there are probably a dozen steps (each one of which is a chance to innovate): from getting customers to realize that it's time to repaint, to helping them choose the color, to shortening the preparation and cleanup time, to keeping track of which colors are on which walls for future reference when it comes time for touch-up.

A journey map helps you think systematically through the steps your customers—internal or external—have when they interact with your product or service. We use maps to synthesize what we learn from interviews and observations. (Or, during field research, you can also try asking your end user to map out his or her own journey.)

TOOL: Customer Journey Map
PARTICIPANTS: Solo or groups of two to six people
TIME: 1–4 hours
SUPPLIES: Whiteboard or Post-its

INSTRUCTIONS

1. Choose a process or journey that you want to map.
2. Write down the steps. Make sure to include even small steps that may seem trivial. The goal is to get you to consider the nuances of the experience that you may normally overlook.
3. Organize the steps into a map. Usually we display the steps sequentially in a timeline. Your map may include branches to show alternative paths in the customer journey. You could also use a series of pictures or whatever method fits your data.
4. Look for insights. What patterns emerge? Anything surprising or strange? Question why certain steps occur, the order they occur in, and so forth. Ask yourself how you might innovate each step.
5. If possible, show the map to people familiar with the journey and ask them what you've overlooked or gotten out of sequence.

TIPS FROM THE FIELD

Here is an example using this method:

Think about a trip to the hospital's emergency room. Of course the most important moment is at the point of care, when the doc is diagnosing the problem or delivering treatment. But when people complain about (or, less commonly, rave about) their emergency room experience, it's not usually the skill of the doctor they are talking about. A simple version of the patient journey might include moments like these:

- Experience pain or discover the symptom.
- Consider home treatment versus going to the hospital: the go/no go decision.
- Choose transportation to the hospital.
- Arrive and park (or pay the taxi, etc.).
- Enter the hospital and find the emergency room.
- See the triage nurse.
- Fill out the insurance forms.
- Wait. And wait some more.
- Get ushered into a treatment room.
- Put on an uncomfortable hospital gown, and wait some more.
- See multiple preliminary nurses and technicians.
- See the doctor for an assessment and sometimes preliminary diagnosis.
- Undergo additional blood tests, X-rays, and so forth.
- Receive a firmer diagnosis, which can lead to getting: instructions for home care, an outpatient procedure, a prescription, a follow-up appointment with a general practitioner or specialist, or admission to the hospital.

As you lay out every step, ask yourself how you might cost-effectively innovate and turn the ordinary experience into something extraordinary.

Because emergency health care is often high-anxiety, we've discovered that patients are calmer if you spell out the journey ahead. We sometimes call that "journifying" the journey—taking an amorphous or scary process and breaking it down into tangible, predictable steps. We've found "journifying" helps people not only in the emergency room, but in any number of health care situations: taking your newborn home from the hospital, going in for surgery, or beginning a new treatment regimen.

DEFINE A PROBLEM TO WORK ON.

Innovators often face the task of which challenge to focus on or how to frame a challenge they are given. At IDEO, we use the term "Phase 0" to describe all the activities that take place before the problem is fully defined.

Talking about problems doesn't necessarily inspire ideas or energize you to act on them. Nor does wishful thinking. The Dream/Gripe Session helps you translate those discussions into creative thinking challenges you can start to tackle. This tool was adapted from an exercise in the *Design Thinking for Educators Toolkit*, developed by IDEO in partnership with Riverdale Country School.

TOOL: The Dream/Gripe Session
PARTICIPANTS: Pairs in groups of any size
TIME: 15–30 minutes
SUPPLIES: Pen and paper

INSTRUCTIONS

1. Decide on a topic for discussion. The dreams and gripes may relate to internal matters like the culture of the organization or external ones like interactions with customers.

2. Pair up with another person and select one person to go first (Partner 1).

3. Partner 1 airs his or her dreams and gripes for five to seven minutes while Partner 2 listens and takes notes.

For example:

DREAM: "I wish we could get our customers to read the instructions."
GRIPE: "It's so noisy around here that I have trouble concentrating."

4. Partner 2 reframes the dreams and gripes into open-ended questions that make for good innovation challenges. We usually start with the phrase "How might we . . . ?" A good "How Might We" question should not be so narrow that it suggests a solution (even if it's a good idea). Initially, you are just trying to capture the problem, not jump to possible solutions. It should also not be so broad that it stymies the flow of ideas (rather than generating them). A good "How Might We" question should allow someone to easily come up with ten different ideas.

   Partner 2 should aim for three to five well-framed innovation challenges and share them with Partner 1.

For example:

GRIPE: It's so noisy around here that I have trouble concentrating.
Challenge that's too similar: How might we reduce noise so you don't have trouble focusing?
Challenge that's too narrow: How might we create more private offices so employees can concentrate better?
Challenge that's too broad: How might we help people focus?
Challenge that's just right: How might we design the space to accommodate a range of working styles?

DREAM: I wish our staff got their expense reports in on time.

Challenge that's too similar: How might we get people to be more timely with their expense reporting?

Challenge that's too narrow: How might we use a smartphone app to speed expense reporting?

Challenge that's too broad: How might we get people to have more respect for deadlines?

Challenge that's just right (with empathy for the employee): How might we simplify the expense reporting process so that people can complete it more quickly?

5. Switch roles and have Partner 2 air dreams and gripes while Partner 1 listens and then offers "How Might We" innovation challenges.

6. (Optional) If you are doing this in a group setting, compare lists of all of the innovation challenges across the pairs. Look for patterns, themes, and common issues. This should help focus the discussion and suggest an opportunity for what innovation challenge to take on next.

If you attend a class or an executive program at the d.school, the first day will most likely include a fast-paced, hands-on activity we call Design Project Zero, or DP0 for short. Rather than try to explain our process for innovation, a DP0 is intended to give people an overview by having them experience it in a microcosm. Faced with a simple innovation challenge, you have a chance to start with empathy, create new ideas, and then build some rapid prototypes, all within about ninety minutes. DP0 projects focus on everything from the gift-giving experience to the ramen-eating experience. The original DP0, explained very briefly here, is called the Wallet Exercise.

The exercise uses a simple object that most people carry with them, as a prop to discover needs, design and prototype solutions, and get user feedback. It gives everyone a chance to cycle quickly through the human-centered design process.

TOOL: The Wallet Exercise

PARTICIPANTS: Pairs in groups of any size

TIME: 90 minutes, plus preparation

SUPPLIES: The facilitator's guide (available on the d.school website [dschool.stanford.edu]) includes a complete list of instructions, worksheets, and prototyping materials. The instructions and worksheets can be printed out for each participant or projected on a screen. Provide prototyping materials (essentially basic craft supplies, which may include markers, colored paper, aluminum foil, tape, pipe cleaners, etc.).

INSTRUCTIONS

1. Participants pair off, with one starting as the interviewer/
   anthropologist, while the other plays the part of the
   prospective customer. The interviewer spends a few minutes
   understanding and empathizing with the other person. The
   interviewee/customer takes out his or her wallet or billfold,
   and they have a discussion about the items inside and the
   meaning attached to them. The interviewer asks questions
   to see how the wallet fits into the customer's life, looking
   especially for problems or friction points associated with
   the wallet. For example: "Have you ever lost your wallet?"
   "Do you use it differently when traveling internationally?"
   "Which items do you take out most often?" After just a few
   minutes, the facilitator calls time, and the team members
   reverse roles, with the interviewer in round one becoming
   the customer in round two.

2. After the participants have had a chance to understand
   the customers and their wallets, the next step is to develop
   a point of view about their latent needs and missed
   opportunities with regard to their wallets. Those need-based
   points of view can take the form of a sentence like "My
   customer needs a way to . . . [user needs] . . . in a way that
   makes them feel . . . [meaning/emotion] . . . because . . .
   [insight]." For example, "My customer needs a way to keep
   track of the contents of their wallet in a way that makes
   them feel secure, because if they lose their wallet, the
   anxiety of not knowing what has gone missing can be worse
   than losing the cash inside."

3. In a form of mini-brainstorming, each participant generates a few concepts for new objects—they may not be physical wallets at all—that satisfy the needs highlighted by the point of view developed in step two.

4. In the most kindergarten-like phase of the wallet exercise, participants create the roughest of prototypes to bring their ideas to life. Using an eclectic mix of materials like construction paper, duct tape, pipe cleaners, and binder clips, the participants will build prototypes just good enough to make their idea tangible so that they can get feedback from their future customer.

5. Using their storytelling skills, a selection of participants "pitch" their new-to-the world wallet concept to their customer and/or to the room at large.

TIPS FROM THE FIELD

The wallet exercise is all about the journey, not the destination. Reading about the wallet exercise doesn't deliver experiential learning. The value is in the doing.

Much of what people take away from this experience happens when debriefing the Wallet Exercise with the whole group. Ask a few pairs to share their prototypes with the larger group. You might ask, "Has anyone's partner come up with a solution so great that you need it right now?" or "Is there an idea so ingenious that it should be backed on Kickstarter?" or "Has someone designed something that is incredibly personal?" Have each pair come up and describe the need they discovered and the prototype they built. Use these shared stories to drive home lessons about empathy, prototyping, getting feedback early and often, and so forth.

This fast-paced format can work for many kinds of challenges. Once you have mastered the Wallet Exercise, think of other innovation challenges to tackle, like redesigning your daily commute or exercise regimen.

MAKING NEW HABITS

Some psychologists claim that you have to practice a new behavior for twenty-one days before it begins to become a habit. The operative word is "practice." The weeks, months, or years spent *thinking* about new behaviors don't count. So pick your favorites from this chapter or create some new experiments of your own. Start accelerating down the runway now if you want your new skills to take flight.

N E x T

EMBRACE CREATIVE CONFIDENCE

Few people think about it or are aware of it. But there is nothing made by human beings that does not involve a design decision somewhere.

—Bill Moggridge

Our great friend and IDEO cofounder Bill Moggridge strongly believed that most people were vastly more creative and capable than they knew. And we have always felt the same way. Societal pressures and corporate norms nudge us toward ideas and behaviors that are "appropriate" or expected. But the rewards for creativity and individuality are well worth the effort. Steve Jobs urged us to do something "insanely great," and during his lifetime that approach allowed him to create and lead one of the most valuable companies in the world. Normalcy is overrated. If you tap into your natural creativity, you have a chance to be extraordinary.

We hope that some of the ideas in *Creative Confidence* will launch you in a new way of thinking. But creative confidence, of course, is not achieved by reading, thinking, or talking about it alone. In our experience, the best way to gain confidence in your creative ability is through action—taken one step at a time—through experiencing a series of small successes. That's what psychologist Albert Bandura found in his research on self-efficacy and guided mastery as well.

The best way to gain confidence in your creative ability is through action—taken one step at a time.

Remember how the first trip down the slide was so scary for young kids, but that fear immediately turned to joy after the first try? We can try to coax and encourage you to start on the journey toward creative confidence, but in the end you are going to have to accept the uncertainty of the path ahead, and just try it and see. Ask yourself, are you willing to start changing your behavior? What action can you take today? What are you prepared to do right now?

One way to think about getting started is to approach building your own creative confidence as your first creative challenge. Think about the innovators you've read about in this book. They all found their own distinct paths to creative confidence:

- Doug Dietz at GE started with empathy, and when he discovered that children feared his beautiful machines, he collected a group of volunteers to create a clever re-design that got at least one patient to say "Mommy, can we come back tomorrow?"

- Biophysics PhD candidate Scott Woody found passion at work, becoming so intensely interested in design-thinking-driven innovation that he abandoned his PhD program and started an entrepreneurial venture.

- Engineers Ankit Gupta and Akshay Kothari, though daunted by the challenge to build a company in ten weeks, took it one step at a time. Embedding themselves in a coffee shop, they adopted a bias toward action and rapidly iterated through prototypes and user testing cycles. The result was Pulse News, an elegantly designed iPad app that has been downloaded by over twenty million people.

- The team behind the Embrace Infant Warmer had to step out of their comfort zone and board a plane to Nepal to learn about low-birth-weight babies. Gaining empathy for all the stakeholders involved, including the mothers and families, sparked insights that led them to reframe their project from a low-cost incubator to an infant warmer.

- Claudia Kotchka organized workshops at P&G that led people through the design thinking process and in so doing gave people a methodology and a little experience so they'd have the confidence to go try it on their own.

Every person's situation is unique. You need to figure out what strategy will work for you. How might you lessen your fear of being judged? How might you better understand the things that hold you back? How might you experiment with different approaches?

NEXT

So set a creative goal, such as capturing at least one new idea or inspiration in a daily journal for the next month. Don't limit yourself—this is a chance to practice deferring judgment, generating wild ideas, going for quantity, and diving into what you value most. Remember that this is just step one. Whatever creative goal you choose, it is important to build on your experience and not let fear and inertia hold you back. Putting ideas on a page and getting past that first hurdle is progress. Then you're ready to take another step forward. Just take it "bird by bird." Pretty soon, you'll start to feel more creative confidence.

Embrace a bias toward action. If you have an idea or active project, try experimenting with the materials on your desk right now to make it more tangible. Or set a goal to build three prototypes for your project this week. You don't have to show them to anyone right away. You can work up to sharing them with your manager or client by sharing them with other people first. In a meeting, when others bring a stack of PowerPoint slides, try using a single image and telling a compelling story. Better yet, bring a prototype or create a simple video that makes your idea come to life. To start even smaller, try to add a sketch to the whiteboard during your next meeting. Or try to go through a whole day without saying "No," instead saying, "Yes, and . . ." or "I could if I . . ."

Executives often claim they have "no budget and no time" for innovation methods. But you don't need to wait for a wad of cash and a big block of time to get started. Instead of letting a lack of resources hold you back, use these constraints to be creative and come up with solutions that require minimal time or money. You may be surprised at how that can spur you on.

Look around you at what you are already doing or what you have to do anyway. Turn it into an opportunity to try a new approach and build your creative confidence. Why not use the time while you're drinking your cup of coffee in the morning to make a bug list? While you're spending time with your kids, practice asking open-ended questions. Instead of asking, "Did you have a good day at school?" try instead asking, "If you were going to tell Grandma about your latest school project, how would you describe it?"

Just as you can gain fluency in a foreign language by speaking it every day—badly at first but with steady progress—developing a creative confidence mindset becomes easier when you practice it regularly. Throughout the book, we've included tools and tactics to help you start making progress. Experiment to see which ones work best for you.

The place to start is with you, as an individual. Even if you ultimately want to instill creative confidence in your group or organization, start by focusing on your own. If you can unleash your creativity and lead by example, it will be much more persuasive than just trying to talk others into changing their behavior.

Here are some strategies to get started with:

SEARCH FOR THE BIG EASY. Tough, daunting challenges tend to deter rather than spark creative action. So start with an easy win, or break down that bigger challenge into more manageable chunks. Outline the individual steps to be taken and look for ways to innovate on each of them. Try focusing your creative energy

NEXT

on a task where progress can take place quickly and you have a good chance of success. What creative project could you tackle by focusing on it for half an hour each day before work?

EXPERIMENT WITH EXPERIENCES. Seek out new experiences. Get another stamp on your passport. Reach out to colleagues at other companies. Or seek out an undiscovered part of your own hometown. Try sitting in the front row at your next big company event (it may seem scary, but it can actually be fun). Pick up a new magazine you've never read before, or spend time on some creative websites. Take a class in the evening—or online. Make a lunch or coffee date with someone new at work. Approach the world with a sense of childlike wonder, and see what new ideas you can identify and explore.

SURROUND YOURSELF WITH A SUPPORTIVE NETWORK. Culture and environment have a big impact on your creative confidence. So surround yourself with like-minded innovators. Find a group to join, online or in person.

Former client Stephanie Rowe used a local community organizing network called Meetup to start a group of her own. After taking a design thinking workshop, she'd been feeling isolated in Washington, DC, and vowed that if she couldn't find kindred spirits locally, she would move to California. What began as a single gathering grew to an active group of over a thousand, dedicated to spreading design thinking. After two decades of experience as an executive, this self-described "hard-core analytical person" says that people have started to tell her, "Wow, you're so creative." To Stephanie, "That is so awesome, but still so odd to hear." She says that creative confidence "has changed my sense of community and what I'm *doing* in my community."

Think about individuals you spend time with at work. Do they tend to reinforce your creativity, or are they skeptics reluctant to consider ideas outside the norm? When you're looking for collaborators, or just for feedback, seek out creative supporters and avoid those whose default mode is negativity. Having partners or colleagues who are also interested in unleashing their creative confidence can be really helpful at this stage.

EXPLORE OPEN INNOVATION COMMUNITIES. No matter where you live, anyone can participate in open innovation platforms. At OpenIDEO, for example, the open innovation platform we know best, you have the chance to contribute at the inspiration, concepting, and evaluation phases of a challenge at whatever level of participation you feel comfortable with. You can express support for other people's ideas by applauding them (a single button click), or you can contribute concepts of your own. You can build on the ideas of others by leaving a comment or uploading a new concept based on another person's initial idea. Every action helps to build your creative confidence, and both big and small contributions to the site get added to your social capital in the form of a "Design Quotient." DQ is intended to help you identify and explore areas where your unique creativity can shine, whether it's at the fuzzy front end of a challenge or in reviewing and evaluating concrete alternatives later on. Open innovation gives you a chance to stretch your creative muscles outside of work. It's great practice you can apply later to your own projects.

NEXT

EMBRACE CONTINUOUS LEARNING. To help build your skills, a coach or a guide can be invaluable. Is there a design thinking workshop you can attend? Check out online resources. For example, IDEO's *Human-Centered Design Toolkit* is a free innovation guide for social enterprises and NGOs. *Design Thinking for Educators* is another toolkit that contains the process and methods of design adapted specifically for the context of K–12 education. The d.school has a *Virtual Crash Course* on its website that leads you through a one-hour innovation workshop in which you redesign an experience like the ritual of gift giving. The site also has a collection of creative methods called the *Bootcamp Bootleg*, which includes some of the tools mentioned in this book.

START DESIGNING YOUR LIFE. Treat the next month of your life as a design project. Do field research on yourself, looking for unmet needs in your own daily routine. Generate ideas about what changes in your behavior might be viable, feasible, and desirable. What improvements can you quickly prototype, test, and iterate? Be intentional about choosing actions you can take right now that might add more joy and meaning to your own life—and the lives of the people around you. How might you work within constraints? Keep iterating. Try this out for a month and ask yourself what's working and what's not. How can you continue to create more positive impact? As our IDEO friend and colleague Tim Brown writes, "Think of today as a prototype. What would you change?"

CREATIVE COMPANIES

The number one question we get when speaking to creative people inside large companies is "How do I convince my boss about these tools?" (And if you *are* the boss, they're talking about you.) Within the constraints of work, company practices, skeptical managers, and quarterly performance pressure, we all have to find a way to make innovation happen. The challenge is to nurture creative behavior in yourself and other team members that will lead to future breakthroughs. We've witnessed a number of successful techniques for navigating corporate cultures:

BUILD ON EXISTING PROCESSES. Sometimes a more gradual change has a higher chance of success than a radical, revolutionary approach.

We talked to one creatively confident person whose first attempt to introduce innovation thinking methods in her aerospace company was a bottom-up "mutiny" involving what she described as "disobedience school" workshops. She had a lot of passion, but the type of change she was suggesting was too much, too fast. Her boss quickly shut it down.

Now, she's taking a different approach with a lot more success. She is fortifying the company's current lean manufacturing process by adding in design thinking methods around field research, idea generation, and prototyping at the front end of new projects. This shift has allowed her to have a positive impact on many projects, from new designs for assembly lines to new ways of doing engineering analysis. "I stopped treating design thinking like it was something separate that people needed to learn, and I just started treating it like it was everyday life," she says. "It's kind of like hiding vegetables in your children's food," she adds. While it might not sound as exciting as a revolution, it's starting to work.

NEXT

DOUBLE DELIVER. If you are struggling to get people on board with your creative approach, remember that even the most dyed-in-the-wool skeptics respond to success. The next time you are given an assignment, give your boss what he or she asked for as you usually do, but in addition try a creative-thinking-oriented alternative. If you end up with a creative solution that works, deliver both to your boss. Be sure to explain that the process was different, as well as the result. The creative solution won't succeed every time, but if you score even a few direct hits, you may win over your management team. And your personal passion will probably be persuasive as well. Once you have a few successes, watch for the moment when your boss starts saying he or she supported the creative approach all along. That's when you know you've won.

A variation on double-delivering is to apply your creative approach to someone *else's* project (while still completing your own work, of course). If you are donating your spare time to another person's project, no one can accuse you of having a hidden agenda. If you fail, it's no loss to your company or colleagues. And if you succeed, you become the quiet hero.

BE REMARKABLE ABOUT THE EXTRACURRICULAR. Volunteer to do extracurricular things, and do them in an extraordinary way. David's former students, now out in the business world, say they've used this approach to thrive in their new organizations. For example, sign up to organize the annual company party or the next management offsite. Start an innovation book club. Host a lunchtime lecture series with visiting experts. Make them a remarkable experience, and everyone will notice. Succeed at a few such visible things, and before long you'll become known as the go-to person for creative thinking. And eventually, you'll be asked to apply your skills to your day-to-day job or a new project or initiative. You'll have the "street cred" you need for such an assignment.

CREATE AN INNOVATION LAB. If you're a manager or leader at your organization, you are in a great position to nurture and grow creative confidence in your company. Dedicate a separate space for innovation; help a small group of innovators transcend the usual practices and constraints and generate new-to-the-world innovations. Apple did it with the Macintosh team. Lockheed did it with their Skunk Works, where they developed exotic aircraft ranging from the U-2 spy plane to the SR-71 Blackbird. Service-oriented retailer Nordstrom has an innovation lab that pops up on the floor of their retail stores. In a single week, they designed, tested, and prototyped an entirely new product from scratch—an iPad app that helps customers pick the perfect pair of sunglasses. Every company needs a lean startup attitude; an innovation lab can help reinforce it.

Does all that sound like a lot of effort? It is. But people have told us that it works. And that they've had a lot of fun along the way, in spite of the work. Or maybe *because* of the work. That is the potential of creative confidence. If you can unleash the creative talent you have carried around inside you since childhood . . . If you can build a few skills and learn a few techniques for applying that creativity . . . If you can find the courage to speak up and experiment, to risk failure and act on your creative impulse . . . you might discover, to paraphrase Noël Coward, that *work* can be more fun than *fun*.

NEXT

So set down this book, or turn off your screen. Pick a first experiment or two, knowing that not all of them will succeed. Start designing your new life. Through effort, practice, and continuous learning, you too can re-imagine your life and career once you embrace creative confidence.

davidkelley@ideo.com
tomkelley@ideo.com

ACKNOWLEDGMENTS

When a movie is over and the credits roll, we are always amazed at how many hands have touched a major film production. And while we didn't use any special effects supervisors or stunt doubles in the production of this book, it *was* a very collaborative project, with literally hundreds of people helping along the way. We'll try to recognize some of the remarkable people who lent us their time and talent over the past few years, knowing in advance that we can't mention everyone . . .

First and foremost, we owe a debt of gratitude to Corina Yen, the young journalist/engineer who joined us in 2011 for what we imagined to be a small role for a short period of time. She ended up doing what seemed like *everything* for almost two years: researching, interviewing, editing, writing, managing the coauthors, and keeping the whole project in her head. Throughout that time, she maintained her urgent optimism—even when we didn't—and kept us on track all the way to completion of the manuscript. We couldn't have done it without her.

Laura McClure joined us for the final and most intense phase of the project, helping us to bring stories to life and converting thoughts into words—all while seemingly unperturbed by the deadline looming larger every day.

We work at the intersection of business and academia and must acknowledge the expert help we got from both of those overlapping worlds.

At IDEO, we got help from people like Chris Flink, who shared many thoughts, read early chapters, and helped us articulate some of IDEO's methodologies. Nicole Kahn helped us put together the "Creative Confidence to Go" activities. CEO Tim Brown and all of our IDEO Partners were continuously supportive of our efforts. Diego Rodriguez volunteered to read through the entire manuscript and give us thoughtful feedback throughout. Other IDEO reviewers included Gabe Kleinman, Colin Raney, and Iain Roberts. Our assistant Kathleen Bomze ran interference for more than two years, often covering for us so that we could get blocks of time open to work on the book.

Martin Kay created the cover design, starting with many prototypes and then narrowing in on one that captured the message and energy we were hoping to express in the book. Beau Bergeron helped us with illustrations in his "spare time," not pausing to so much as take a breath from his client work. Fabian Herrmann helped us design the book's interior. Alana Zawojski and Katie Clark helped us corral the photos and other images into place. Brendan Boyle was a good sounding board as our ideas emerged and a frequent contributor when we needed a playful idea or a relevant example. Whitney Mortimer, Debbe Stern, and their entire Marcom team supported us through the completion of the manuscript and beyond.

And then there are the 600 people of the firm who practice design thinking and embrace creative confidence every day. They told us stories, shared insights, and responded to our All-IDEO email questions with prolific answers. We'd especially like to thank the IDEOers who stopped by our project space in the final weeks to help with specific spots where we needed fresh thought: Dennis Boyle, Brian Mason, Jonah Houston, Grace Hwang, and IDEO.org founders Patrice Martin and Jocelyn Wyatt. Others too numerous to mention include contributors like Tom Hulme, Joerg Student,

David Haygood, Coe Leta Stafford, Mark Jones, Joe Wilcox, and Stacey Chang.

At the same time, we got lots of help and support from our friends at the d.school. Managing Director Sarah Stein Greenberg and Executive Director George Kembel not only gave us ideas for the book, but also covered for David in a thousand ways during this project. Bob Sutton, who has always traded ideas back and forth with us, was the first person we interviewed and pointed us toward many more. Bernie Roth has supported the d.school from the very beginning and gave us more creative confidence stories than we could fit into the book. Perry Klebahn and Jeremy Utley have helped translate ideas from the d.school for executive audiences and helped us think about both academia and business. Scott Doorley has been a thought leader about how space affects culture, and we built on his thoughts about creative groups. A special thanks also to Bill Burnett, executive director of the Stanford Design Program, for the leadership that freed up David's time to work on this book. And thanks to the many others who contributed stories, ideas, and inspiration.

Beyond IDEO and the d.school, there were still dozens of others who helped us with their thoughts, words, and actions. Albert Bandura was an important early inspiration, and his deep research sustained us along the way. Carol Dweck altered our worldview through her written work and when we met in person. Catherine Fredman was a friend in need, offering her professional editorial advice at times when the project seemed like it might stall out. Reviewers Nancy Martin from GE, Carl Roetter from 3M, Bill Leigh from the Leigh Bureau, and long-time friend Jim Manzi gave us objective feedback about the manuscript—including tough love where they felt we needed additional work.

And to the 100+ people we interviewed about their own creative confidence journey—from Marcy Barton to Claudia Kotchka to Bonny Simi—we found all of your stories inspiring. We deeply appreciate your generosity in sharing your experiences and insights.

In the publishing world, we want to particularly thank literary agent Christy Fletcher for getting us this far, and our editor, Roger Scholl at Crown Business, for believing in us once again.

A very special thanks to Dr. Dimitrios Colevas, Dr. Michael J. Kaplan, and the staff of Stanford Hospital, who helped David beat the long odds on cancer in 2007 so that this book could come to life.

And most of all, thanks to our wives, Yumi and Kc—as well as our kids—for being supportive and patient throughout a project that was longer than anyone expected.

Thanks, everyone! We hope you're happy with the book you helped to make.

NOTES

INTRODUCTION

2   ***Disabling hearing loss:*** Statistic is from the World Health Organization, "Deafness and Hearing Loss," February 2013, http://www.who.int/media centre/factsheets/fs300/en.

3   ***"Do Schools Kill Creativity?":*** Everyone should watch the inspiring TED Talk by Sir Ken Robinson. "Do Schools Kill Creativity," February 2006, http://www.ted.com/talks/ken_robinson_says schools_kill_creativity .html. As of November 2012, it was the most watched TED talk to date (http://blog.ted.com/2012/08/21/the-20-most-watched-ted-talks-to-date).

4   ***IBM survey:*** IBM, press release, May 18, 2010, http://www-03.ibm.com/ press/us/en/pressrelease/31670.wss.

4   ***Adobe Systems poll:*** Adobe Systems, press release, April 23, 2012, http:// www.adobe.com/aboutadobe/pressroom/pressreleases/201204/042312Ado beGlobalCreativityStudy.html.

6   ***Tibetan language:*** We have talked multiple times with Geshe Thupten Jinpa about empathy and compassion. Our conversation about creative confidence and the "natural" state of creativity took place in September 2010 while he was staying in David's guesthouse.

7   ***People who have embraced creative confidence:*** These thumbnail sketches of individuals refer to Bonny Simi, David Hughes, Lauren Weinstein, Stephanie Rowe, and Marcy Barton. Their stories come from interviews conducted by Corina Yen and Tom Kelley (see notes on their full stories in subsequent chapters). JetBlue's 40 percent accelerated recovery time was reported by Dan Heath and Chip Heath in "Team Coordination Is Key in Businesses," *Fast Company*, July/August 2010, http://www .fastcompany.com/1659112/team-coordination-key-businesses. Over 1,700 people signed the petition circulated by Hughes's team or joined their Facebook group, as reported in a blog post from the *Harvard Business Review*. (See Julia Kirby, "Starting a Movement, Learning to Lead," June 1, 2009, http://blogs.hbr.org/hbr/hbreditors/2009/06/starting_a_movement_ learning_t.html.)

9   ***Executive recruiters:*** One of the first people we know to use design

thinking in the world of executive recruiting is Ben Anderson of Renaissance Leadership Ltd., http://www.ren-lead.com.

9   *Social workers:* See, for example, the story of Phil Ansell, a director of the Los Angeles County Department of Public Social Services, on the d.school's blog, *Design + Bureaucracy = Delight,* November 13, 2012, http://dschool.stanford.edu/blog/2012/11/13/design-bureaucracy-delight.

10   *"Self-efficacy":* Albert Bandura, *Self-Efficacy: The Exercise of Control* (New York: W. H. Freeman, 1997).

CHAPTER 1

13   *GE Healthcare, an $18 billion division:* Kate Linebaugh, "GE Feels Its Own Cuts," September 17, 2012, *Wall Street Journal,* http://online.wsj.com/article/SB10000872396390443720204578002270222435846.html.

13   *MRI machine:* We first heard Doug Dietz's story in a video taken at a d.school Executive Education Bootcamp class in July 2011. You can hear Doug tell his own story in his TEDx Talk. See Dietz, "Transforming Healthcare for Children and Their Families," April 2012, http://tedxtalks.ted.com/video/TEDxSanJoseCA-2012-Doug-Dietz-T. Other details come from an interview with Doug by Corina Yen and Tom Kelley in November 2011.

22   *Design-Driven Innovation:* Thanks to IDEO partner and d.school consulting associate professor Chris Flink for his help articulating the design thinking process. For further reading on design thinking, we recommend IDEO CEO Tim Brown's book *Change by Design.* For tools and techniques, check out IDEO's free online resources like the *Human-Centered Design Toolkit* (http://www.hcdconnect.org/toolkit/en) and the *Design Thinking for Educators Toolkit* (http://designthinkingforeducators.com/toolkit). The d.school also shares its methods online in formats that include the *Bootcamp Bootleg* toolkit (see link at http://dschool.stanford.edu/use-our-methods).

25   **The Art of Innovation:** Tom's first book tells the early history of IDEO and provides a look into our process at that time. Tom Kelley with Jonathan Littman, *The Art of Innovation: Lessons in Creativity from IDEO, America's Leading Design Firm* (New York: Doubleday, 2001).

30   *"Growth mindset":* See Carol Dweck, *Mindset: The New Psychology of Success* (New York: Random House, 2006), 7. Her work first caught our eye in an article by Marina Krakovsky, "The Effort Effect," *Stanford Magazine,* March/April 2007, http://alumni.stanford.edu/get/page/magazine/article/?article_id=32124. Beyond her book, additional details came from an interview with Carol Dweck by Corina Yen and David and Tom Kelley

in September 2011. Dweck's research was very thought-provoking for us, influencing everything from how we think about creativity to how we talk with our own kids.

31   ***Studying the behavior of freshman:*** See Dweck, *Mindset*, 17–18.

34   ***"You can poke life":*** You can find the inspiring clip of Steve Jobs being interviewed in 1994 by the Silicon Valley Historical Association online at http://www.youtube.com/watch?v=kYfNvmF0Bqw. Some of the other material related to Steve was drawn from the twenty-five-year friendship between him and David.

CHAPTER 2

37   ***Picture a boa constrictor:*** The phobia cure story was told to David by Albert Bandura in a September 2010 interview. More details were drawn from a retelling of the experiment in Kerry Patterson et al., *Influencer: The Power to Change Anything* (New York: McGraw-Hill, 2007), 47–48. For more about self-efficacy and guided mastery see Albert Bandura, *Self-Efficacy: The Exercise of Control* (New York: W. H. Freeman, 1997).

37   ***Greatest living psychologist:*** Christine Foster, "Confidence Man," *Stanford Magazine*, September/October 2006, http://alumni.stanford.edu/get/page/magazine/article/?article_id=33332.

37   ***Only Sigmund Freud:*** Bandura was ranked fourth on the list by Steven J. Haggbloom, in "The 100 Most Eminent Psychologists of the 20th Century," *Review of General Psychology* 6, no. 2 (2002): 139–52.

38   ***Dream about a boa constrictor:*** Bandura, *Self-Efficacy*, 150.

39   ***People mentioned other changes:*** Bandura, *Self-Efficacy*, 53.

40   ***Creative people simply do more experiments:*** Dean Keith Simonton, *Origins of Genius: Darwinian Perspectives on Creativity* (New York: Oxford University Press, 1999). Thanks to Stanford professor of management science and engineering Bob Sutton, who first told us about Simonton's research on creative geniuses.

41   ***Remote Outer Banks location:*** The Wright brothers appeared as larger-than-life figures in the Ohio history courses of our childhood. The idea that they picked Kitty Hawk partly to avoid media attention came from Wikipedia, accessed February 22, 2013, http://en.wikipedia.org/wiki/Wright_brothers.

42   ***Reinvent the traditional classroom chair:*** The Node Chair was a Steelcase/IDEO project completed in 2010. Details about the prototypes came from IDEO designer Joerg Student and from Steelcase's General Manager of Education Solutions, Sean Corcorran, in e-mails and conver-

sations during April 2013. The number of institutions using the chairs as of spring 2013 was supplied by Steelcase. For more about the Node project, go to http://www.ideo.com/work/node-chair.

43   ***Gift-giving experience:*** You can try doing the ninety-minute gift-giving project yourself following instructions on the d.school website, https://dschool.stanford.edu/groups/designresources/wiki/ed894/The_GiftGiving _Project.html. The gift-giving project is a good demonstration of how to apply the design cycle to an experience (rather than a physical product).

43   ***Daily commute:*** Improving the daily commute experience (specifically the Caltrain commute between Palo Alto and San Francisco) is a popular project at the d.school. Students look at the whole customer journey: waiting on the platform, riding the train, finding your way when you get out in the station, talking to the people on the train, enjoying the ride, getting food, and so forth.

43   ***"Failure sucks, but instructs":*** Bob Sutton and IDEO partner and d.school consulting associate professor Diego Rodriguez started using this expression after teaching their first class at the d.school, Creating Infectious Action. As Bob wrote on his blog, *Work Matters,* "We preached [a]bout failing forward, failing early and failing often, and used a host of other pretty words to talk about the good things that happen when things go badly. . . . So after our students—under our guidance—were especially unsuccessful at promoting a hip-hop concert . . . we realized that the most honest thing to do was . . . to talk about how much it sucked to have such a lousy outcome, and then turn to the learning." See "Failure Sucks but Instructs," October 29, 2007, http://bobsutton.typepad.com/my_weblog/2007/10/failure-sucks-b.html. Diego made the phrase number fourteen in a series of twenty-one principles of innovation posted on his blog: "14: Failure sucks, but instructs," May 20, 2009, http://metacool.com/?p=324.

44   ***"Many d.school classes demand":*** This quote from Chris Flink comes from an internal d.school document. It was part of a point-of-view statement for thinking about the future of the d.school.

44   ***"The Drop":*** John "Cass" Cassidy has been a frequent visitor to IDEO in the past decade or two and has been a role model in how to encourage creative confidence in others. See John Cassidy and B. C. Rimbeaux, *Juggling for the Complete Klutz* (Palo Alto, CA: Klutz, 2007), 4. Also check out *The Klutz Book of Invention* by Cass and Brendan Boyle, a compendium of brilliant yet ridiculous product ideas.

45   ***Overcoming Fear of Customer Interviews:*** Thanks to d.school lecturer Caroline O'Connor and managing director Sarah Stein Greenberg

for their help with this sidebar. The material was adapted from ideas that first appeared in a similar sidebar they contributed to an article we wrote for *Harvard Business Review*, "Reclaim Your Creative Confidence," December 2012, 116–17.

47   **Power of video games:** See Jane McGonigal, *Reality Is Broken: Why Games Make Us Better and How They Can Change the World* (New York: Penguin Press, 2011). The chapter that is most relevant to creative confidence, "Fun Failure and Better Odds of Success," demonstrates how failure is reframed in a gaming context. The definition of urgent optimism comes from Jane's first compelling TED Talk, "Gaming can make a better world," February 2010, http://www.ted.com/talks/jane_mcgonigal_gaming_can_make _a_better_world.html. Additional details come from two conversations between Jane and Tom in November 2012.

49   **"Mileage":** This is one of Diego Rodriguez's innovation principles described on his blog: "It's not the years, it's the mileage," August 12, 2009, http://metacool.com/?p=297.

49   **"Constructive failure":** Randy Komisar talked about constructive failure in a lecture recorded at Stanford in April 2004, posted online by the Stanford Technology Ventures Program Entrepreneurship Corner, http:// ecorner.stanford.edu/authorMaterialInfo.html?mid=996. For more about Randy's thoughts on risk and failure see Randy Komisar with Kent Lineback, *Monk and the Riddle: The Education of a Silicon Valley Entrepreneur* (Boston: Harvard Business School Press, 2000).

49   **Reinventing European venture capital:** The HackFWD project was completed by IDEO for Lars Hinrichs in 2010; see http://www.ideo.com/ work/hackfwd. You can get a copy of the Geek Agreement from the HackFWD website, http://hackfwd.com/experience.

50   **Ninety-seven such innovative ventures:** The number of funded projects is as reported in Alexander Eule, "Forever in Blue Jeans," *Barron's,* February 23, 2013, http://online.barrons.com/article/SB50001424052748 704103204578314212712289502.htm.

52   **"Anti-Portfolio":** Thanks to Chris Flink for first telling us about Bessemer's "Anti-Portfolio." You can see the entire list at http://www.bvp.com/ portfolio/antiportfolio.

52   **Forbes *Midas List*:** In 2013, David Cowan was number sixty-one. See http://www.forbes.com/midas/list.

52   **Failure conferences:** FailCon is an annual conference that started in San Francisco in 2009 and now holds international events as well. See http:// thefailcon.com.

52   *Failure résumé:* Tina Seelig, *What I Wish I Knew When I Was 20: A Crash Course on Making Your Place in the World* (New York: HarperOne, 2009), 71–73.

55   *"Creativity scar":* Brené Brown, *Daring Greatly: How the Courage to Be Vulnerable Transforms the Way We Live, Love, Parent, and Lead* (New York: Gotham Books, 2012), 189–90.

55   *Traditional schooling destroys creativity:* The first quote comes from Sir Ken Robinson's TED Talk, "Do Schools Kill Creativity?" For the second quote, see Sir Ken Robinson and Lou Aronica, *The Element: How Finding Your Passion Changes Everything* (New York: Viking Press, 2009), 16.

56   *Paul McCartney:* Sir Ken Robinson told this story to David and Tom in December 2010. Sir Ken has also written about it in Robinson and Aronica, *The Element*, 9–11, 228. For details about the history of the Liverpool Institute for Performing Arts see http://www.lipa.ac.uk/content/About Us/HistoryHeritage.aspx (accessed January 11, 2011).

57   *Research on insecurity:* See Brené Brown, *The Gifts of Imperfection: Let Go of Who You Think You're Supposed to Be and Embrace Who You Are* (Center City, MN: Hazelden, 2010), 94–97. Brown describes her research methodology and number of interviewees on page 129. The quote is from Brown, *Daring Greatly*, 64.

58   *Research on resilience:* See Brown's summary of resilience research in *The Gifts of Imperfection*, 63–76.

59   *Expert on the art of visual thinking:* Dan Roam, *The Back of the Napkin: Solving Problems and Selling Ideas with Pictures* (New York: Portfolio, 2009). The description of "red pen" and "yellow pen" people is on pages 24–25. Some details come from a conversation between Dan and Tom in January 2012. You can check out the Napkin Academy at http://www.napkin academy.com.

60   *Sketching People:* Thanks to Dan Roam for drawing these illustrations. The description is based on his "How to Draw People" lesson in Roam's "Napkin Academy," http://www.napkinacademy.com/how-to-draw-people.

CHAPTER 3

67   *Embrace Infant Warmer:* Corina Yen and Tom interviewed Rahul Panicker about this story in October 2011. Rahul's remarks throughout the story come from the interview, unless otherwise noted. Some details come from a conversation between Jane Chen and David in February 2013. Details about the cost of the product come from Embrace's website, http://www.embraceglobal.org.

68   ***Fifteen million premature and low-birth-weight babies:*** Statistics are from the World Health Organization, "Preterm Birth," November 2012, http://www.who.int/mediacentre/factsheets/fs363/en/index.html.

68   ***"These babies are so tiny":*** Sean Dooley, "Embrace Infant Warmer Could Save Thousands," *ABC News,* December 17, 2010, http://abcnews.go.com/Health/embrace-infant-warmer-save-thousands/story?id=12366774.

69   ***"That's going to be hard":*** The story and quotes are from video of an interview with Embrace team members produced by Corey Ford for the d.school, online at http://vimeo.com/11283910.

72   ***One of the original team members:*** Embrace cofounder Razmig Hovaghimian stayed on as a board member.

72   ***"Philosophy of Embrace":*** Dooley, "Embrace Infant Warmer."

72   ***ABC News show 20/20:*** "Be the Change: The Tiniest Survivors," December 17, 2010, http://abcnews.go.com/2020/video/change-tiniest-survivors-12428134?&clipId=12428134&playlistId=12428134.

73   ***"Time and capital it would require":*** Jane Chen, "Should Your Business Be Nonprofit or For-Profit?" *HBR Blog Network,* February 1, 2013, http://blogs.hbr.org/cs/2013/02/should_your_business_be_nonpro.html. Data about the number of babies helped and other details about the status of the company are also from this post.

75   ***They decided to be creative:*** Robert Sternberg, interview by Corina Yen and Tom Kelley, November 2011. The list of attributes is from Sternberg, "The WICS Approach to Leadership: Stories of Leadership and the Structure and Processes That Support Them," *Leadership Quarterly* 19, no. 3 (2008): 360–71. The quote is from Sternberg, "Creativity as a Decision," *American Psychologist,* May 2002, 376. Thanks to Bob Sutton for first bringing Sternberg's work to our attention.

76   ***Piñata cookies:*** Jill Levinsohn, interview by Corina Yen, September 2012. You can check out Jill's Pinterest page at http://pinterest.com/jml736.

78   ***Passengers sitting alone:*** This example comes from IDEO designer Kerry O'Connor, who has been a coach in many d.school executive education classes.

79   ***Make a Community Chalkboard:*** Thanks to Alan Ratliff, a leader in IDEO's experience team, for his help with this sidebar. He sparked the idea for it in our San Francisco office after getting inspired by a Santa Cruz bathroom with chalkboard graffiti.

81   ***Cool News of the Day:*** Tim Manners started writing this daily newsletter one morning in 1998, just for fun, and never stopped. Tom met Tim when they worked together on Seth Godin's group-effort book, *The Big Moo,* and

has subscribed to *Cool News* ever since. Check it out at http://www.reveries .com.

81 **Great Ormond Street Hospital:** See Gautam Naik, "A Hospital Races to Learn Lessons of Ferrari Pit Stop," *Wall Street Journal,* November 14, 2006, http://online.wsj.com/article/SB116346916169622261.html.

82 **"Abundance mentality":** See Stephen Covey, *The Seven Habits of Highly Effective People* (New York: Simon & Schuster, 1989), 219–20.

83 **Jonathan Schooler:** See John Tierney, "Discovering the Virtues of a Wandering Mind," *New York Times,* June 28, 2010, D1.

83 **"Relaxed attention":** See Robert H. McKim, *Experiences in Visual Thinking* (Pacific Grove, CA: Brooks/Cole, 1980), 38. Another book about creativity that was influential for David early on is Don Koberg and Jim Bagnall, *The Universal Traveler: A Soft-Systems Guide to Creativity, Problem-Solving, and the Process of Reaching Goals* (Los Altos, CA: William Kaufmann, 1974).

86 **"Anthropology is too important":** Tom introduced Grant McCracken's talk, "Who Owns Culture in the Corporation?" at the AIGA Business and Design Conference 2008 when he said this quote: http://www.aiga.org/ resources/content/5/3/2/3/documents/aiga_gain08_mccracken.pdf.

86 **PNC Financial Services:** This story was told to us by IDEO's Chicago location head Mark Jones in an interview by Corina Yen and David Kelley in March 2012. For more information about the project go to http://www .ideo.com/work/virtual-wallet-interactive-banking-experience.

86 **Fourteen thousand new customers:** See Nicola Trevett, "The Big Broken Bank Rebuild," *Guardian,* March 12, 2010, http://www.guardian .co.uk/service-design/bank-rebuild.

87 **Six million people:** 2013 Fact Sheet available on the PNC website, https://www.pnc.com/webapp/sec/NCProductsAndService.do?siteArea=/ pnccorp/PNC/Home/About+PNC/Media+Room/PNC+Fact+Sheets.

87 **$30 billion a year:** This figure comes from a study by economic research firm Moebs Services. See "A Further Look at Overdraft Fees," *New York Times,* February 27, 2012, http://www.nytimes.com/2012/02/27/ opinion/a-further-look-at-overdraft-fees.html. A 2008 study by the Federal Deposit Insurance Corporation found that nearly 50 percent of young adult account holders incurred overdraft fees and were the most likely age group to incur them. "FDIC Study of Bank Overdraft Programs," November 2008, http://www.fdic.gov/bank/analytical/overdraft/FDIC138 _Report_Final_v508.pdf.

88 **"I'm just out of college":** Burt Helm, "PNC Lures Gen Y with Its

'Virtual Wallet' Account," *Businessweek*, November 25, 2008, http://www. businessweek.com/stories/2008-11-25/pnc-lures-gen-y-with-its-virtual -wallet-account.

88   ***"Begin projects with customers"*:** Quoted in Frederick S. Leichter, "How Fidelity Used Design Thinking to Perfect Its Website," *HBR Blog Network,* May 9, 2011, http://blogs.hbr.org/cs/2011/05/how_fidelity_used _design_think.html.

89   ***Hybrid Insights:*** IDEO design researcher Juliette Melton sat down with Corina Yen and Tom in October 2012 to tell us about hybrid insights. To learn more about it, see Johannes Seemann, "Hybrid Insights: Where the Quantitative Meets the Qualitative," *Rotman* magazine, Fall 2012, 56–61.

90   ***Ice-cream scoops:*** IDEO senior lead Brian Mason told this story to Tom in February 2013. For more about the Zyliss project, go to http://www.ideo .com/work/kitchen-gadgets.

91   ***Future of beauty care:*** This story and details come from a design research video taken during IDEO's fieldwork on that project.

92   ***LittleMissMatched:*** Details about LittleMissMatched come from e-mails and company presentations shared with Tom by the company's founder, Jonah Staw. The image included with the story is a reenactment.

94   ***"I walked into the room"*:** Amanda Sammann, interview by Corina Yen and Tom Kelley, April 2012.

96   ***Asking questions of potential end users:*** Coe Leta Stafford is a resident expert on interviewing and design research. She shared these tips with Tom in an e-mail on February 21, 2012.

97   ***Interview techniques:*** See IDEO's *Human-Centered Design Toolkit,* http:// www.hcdconnect.org/toolkit/en.

99   ***"Improve videoconferencing"*:** CEO John Chambers presented this reframing example to an IDEO team during a project we worked on with Cisco.

99   ***Tools for sinus surgery:*** Details of this story about the Gyrus Diego Powered Dissector System were checked by IDEO partner Andrew Burroughs, who led the IDEO project team that worked on it. For more about the project, go to http://www.ideo.com/work/diego-powered-dissector -system.

100   ***8 percent of students:*** William G. Bowen, Martin Kurzweil, and Eugene Tobin, *Equity and Excellence in American Higher Education* (Charlottesville: University of Virginia Press, 2005), 91, as cited by David Brooks in *The Social Animal.*

102   ***Drinking the impure water:*** Details of this story about the Ripple Effect

project were checked by IDEO's Sally Madsen, who led the IDEO project team that worked on it. For more about the project go to http://www.ideo .com/work/ripple-effect-access-to-safe-drinking-water.

102 **Community Action Project:** Jocelyn Wyatt and Patrice Martin, interview by Tom Kelley, February 2013. For more about the project, go to https:// www.ideo.org/projects/breaking-the-cycle-of-intergenerational-poverty/ completed.

104 **Advisory boards:** See Keith Ferrazzi, *Who's Got Your Back: The Break-through Program to Build Deep, Trusting Relationships That Create Success—And Won't Let You Fail* (New York: Crown Business, 2009), 60–62.

105 **Charles Goodyear:** This story was told and retold in the Ohio history classes of our childhood. For more of the story, see Goodyear's website, www.goodyear.com/corporate/history/history_story.html.

CHAPTER 4

109 **Akshay Kothari or Ankit Gupta:** Akshay and Ankit's story and quotes are based primarily on an interview with them conducted by Corina Yen and Tom Kelley in October 2011. A few additional details come from a conversation between Corina and Akshay in May 2013.

116 **Working prototype of a service:** The story and details about John's prototype come from a post John wrote on his blog, "Where's the Next Bus? I'll Tell You," April 2011, http://johnkeefe.net/wheres-the-next-bus-ill -tell-you.

116 **"The most effective way":** See 2012 d.school fact sheet, http://dschool .stanford.edu/wp-content/uploads/2010/09/dschool-fact-sheet-2012.pdf.

117 **Morning news show:** The show that was in development, now called *The Takeaway*, was launched in 2008. The class was Media + Design, taught by d.school creative director Scott Doorley. Prototypes from students were put on the air during WNYC's *The Brian Lehrer Show*.

118 **Bug list:** You can read more about bug lists in Tom's book *The Art of Innovation* (pp. 28–31).

119 **"Knowing-doing gap":** See Jeffrey Pfeffer and Robert I. Sutton, *The Knowing-Doing Gap: How Smart Companies Turn Knowledge into Action* (Boston: Harvard Business School Press, 1999).

119 **Kodak:** Our story about missed opportunities at Kodak began with a visit to the company's headquarter in April 1997. We have followed the company's ups and downs ever since. Kodak's peak market share data varied by product category. See, for example, Andrew Martin, "Negative Exposure for Kodak," *New York Times*, October 20, 2011, http://www.nytimes

.com/2011/10/21/business/kodaks-bet-on-its-printers-fails-to-quell-the-doubters.html.

121 **Bernie Roth:** Many students from the d.school's Summer College told us about Bernie's exercise. The stories of those spurred to action were reported to us by the d.school's Director of Community, Charlotte Burgess-Auburn, who helps with Summer College, in an e-mail on January 5, 2012.

122 *"We were out at our family cabin":* Anne Lamott, *Bird by Bird: Some Instructions on Writing and Life* (New York: Anchor Books, 1995), 18–19. We recommend the whole book as well for advice on pursuing creative endeavors in general.

123 **Clever ceramics instructor:** The pottery fable is told in David Bayles and Ted Orland, *Art & Fear* (Santa Cruz, CA: Image Continuum Press, 2001), 29. The book is a fast read and inspiring for more than just artists.

124 *"Most of us have two lives":* See Steven Pressfield, *The War of Art: Break through the Blocks and Win Your Creative Battles* (New York: Black Irish Entertainment, 2002). Quotes are from the opening section, "The Unlived Life." Our friend Ben Anderson lent us his copy of Pressfield's *The War of Art.* There is a lot of "resistance" in a multiyear book project, and we found the concept very useful.

127 **Executive education workshop:** Jeremy Utley, interview by David Kelley and Corina Yen, August 2011. Jeremy has led many sessions at the d.school as director of executive education.

127 **Francis Ford Coppola:** The taxi story comes from a conversation Tom had with Francis Ford Coppola backstage at an HSM ExpoManagement event in Buenos Aires in November 2007. The low-budget film was *Youth Without Youth.* More of Coppola's thoughts on the film and financing it himself were captured in an article in *Vanity Fair,* at http://www.vanityfair.com/culture/features/2007/12/coppola200712.

128 **Ways to use constraints:** Constrained voting and creating a "drumbeat" are two common practices at IDEO that IDEO partner Dennis Boyle discussed with Tom in an interview in February 2013.

130 **Prototyping:** To learn more about prototyping at IDEO and elsewhere, see Tom's previous books, for example, *The Art of Innovation,* chapter 6, and Tom Kelley with Jonathan Littman, *The Ten Faces of Innovation* (New York: Doubleday, 2005), chapter 2.

130 **Minimum viable product:** Eric is an IDEO Fellow, and his book is a useful guide for those with an entrepreneurial spirit. Eric Ries, *The Lean Startup: How Today's Entrepreneurs Use Continuous Innovation to Create Radically Successful Businesses* (New York: Crown Business, 2011).

132 *Elmo's Monster Maker:* Adam Skaates told this story to Tom in December 2011. Check out the original video Adam and Coe Leta made at http://youtu.be/-SOeMA3DUEs.

133 *Boyle's Law:* Tom first talked about Boyle's Law and its creator, Dennis Boyle, in *The Art of Innovation* (p. 106). The name is borrowed—with apologies—from the more famous Boyle's Law you may have heard about in physics class. That one came from Irish physicist Robert Boyle.

134 *Tips for Quick Videos:* We completely believe in the power of a video to paint a picture of the future and quickly get your point across. IDEO partner Brendan Boyle and the Toy Lab, who are masters of the technique, put these tips together.

136 *Walgreens:* The story about the Walgreens project and the foam core prototype came from an interview with Mark Jones, who led that project, conducted by Corina Yen and David in March 2012. There was also a follow-up conversation between Mark and Corina Yen in May 2012. Some of the details came from the project description on the IDEO website, http://www.ideo.com/work/community-pharmacy.

137 *Quadrupled the number of customers:* These results and data on the number of stores with the new format were reported to us by Walgreens in an e-mail on May 7, 2013.

138 *Innovative U.S. health care companies:* Walgreens was included in *Fast Company*'s list of Most Innovative Companies in the Health Care industry for 2012 and 2013 (as well as 2010).

138 *Storyboarding a service:* For more details about storyboarding, you can also look at the *Design Thinking for Educators* toolkit, http://designthinkingforeducators.com/toolkit.

139 *Write three questions:* This tip comes from IDEO partner Peter Coughlan. He says that the technique makes you less afraid to articulate your idea. He says, "It gives you the opportunity to appear less dumb by asking further questions that you know your storyboard couldn't have answered."

140 *"The world's longest hauls":* "Long-Haul Travel Experience for Air New Zealand," IDEO website, http://www.ideo.com/work/long-haul-travel-experience.

140 *"I am quite comfortable":* Divina Paredes, "Flight Path to CEO," *CIO*, April 10, 2008, http://cio.co.nz/cio.nsf/spot/flight-path-to-ceo.

141 *"It was liberating":* Geoffrey Thomas, "Reinventing Comfort," *Air Transport World*, February 1, 2010, http://atwonline.com/operations-maintenance/article/reinventing-comfort-0309.

142 *"Launch to learn":* We first heard about "launch to learn" from IDEO

design director Tom Hulme in an interview by Corina Yen and Tom Kelley in July 2011. We thank him for pointing us toward the Zynga and Kindle lending examples.

142 **Half a billion dollars:** Statistics about Kickstarter come from their website, http://www.kickstarter.com/help/stats.

143 **"Ghetto testing":** Hear more about how Zynga does "ghetto testing" from founder Mark Pincus in a talk recorded in October 2009 at Stanford, posted online by the Stanford Technology Ventures Program Entrepreneurship Corner, http://ecorner.stanford.edu/authorMaterialInfo.html?mid=2277.

143 **Lending feature for Kindle books:** Audrey Waters, "New Kindle Lending Club Matches E-Book Borrowers and Lenders," *ReadWrite*, January 15, 2011, http://readwrite.com/2011/01/15/new_kindle_lending_club_matches_e-book_borrowers_a.

143 **"Release your idea":** Tom Hulme, "Launch Your Next Idea Before It's Ready," *HBR Blog Network* [video], August 28, 2012, http://blogs.hbr.org/video/2012/08/launch-your-next-idea-before-i.html.

144 **Pedestrian mall:** David Hughes, interview by Corina Yen, September 2011. Additional details from Julia Kirby, "Starting a Movement, Learning to Lead," *HBR Blog Network*, June 1, 2009, http://blogs.hbr.org/hbr/hbreditors/2009/06/starting_a_movement_learning_t.html. This story was first brought to our attention by Bob Sutton, who started the Creating Infectious Action class along with Diego Rodriguez. David Hughes's teammates on the pedestrian mall project were Amrita Mahale, James Thompson, and Svetla Alexandrov.

146 **Steelcase open-air Leadership Community:** This story came from conversations with Jim Hackett during the creation of the community (1994) and from witnessing the space in action during the ensuing years. Some details were confirmed via e-mails with Jim in March 2013.

146 **"Most analytical people":** Conversation between Akshay Kothari and Corina Yen, May 2013.

CHAPTER 5

151 **Economic research:** Derek Thompson, "The 10 Things Economics Can Tell Us About Happiness," *Atlantic*, May 31, 2012, http://www.theatlantic.com/business/archive/2012/05/the-10-things-economics-can-tell-us-about-happiness/257947.

152 **"Chinese finger traps":** Robert Sternberg, interview by Corina Yen and Tom Kelley, November 2011.

153 *Jeremy found himself trapped:* Jeremy Utley, interview by Corina Yen and David Kelley, August 2011.

155 *A job, a career, or a calling:* Amy Wrzesniewski et al. "Jobs, Careers, and Callings: People's Relations to Their Work," *Journal of Research in Personality*, 31, no. 1 (1997): 21–33. We first encountered her work in Jonathan Haidt, *The Happiness Hypothesis: Finding Modern Truth in Ancient Wisdom* (New York: Basic Books, 2006), 221–23.

157 *Switched from fixing problems:* Conversations with Jane Fulton Suri in 1991 (details verified by Jane in December 2012).

158 *Drudgery and effort of practicing:* Erik Moga, interview by Tom Kelley, October 2011.

158 *"I'd work by myself":* Scott Woody, interview by Corina Yen, August 2011. Thanks to d.school director of executive education Perry Klebahn for pointing us toward his LaunchPad alumnus.

159 *d.school studio class:* Creative Gym was created and is taught by Charlotte Burgess-Auburn, Grace Hawthorne, and Scott Doorley of the d.school.

162 *Three overlapping circles:* See Jim Collins, *Good to Great: Why Some Companies Make the Leap . . . and Others Don't* (New York: HarperBusiness, 2001), 94–97. Jim first talks about the three circles as the "Hedgehog Concept" and applies it to what makes a great company.

162 *"Flow":* We highly recommend Mihaly Csikszentmihalyi's work, including *Creativity: Flow and the Psychology of Discovery and Invention* (New York: Harper Perennial, 1997).

165 *Knowledge-sharing sessions:* IDEOer Andy Switky is the cheese aficionado of the office. Elysa Fenenbock is the jewelry designer who is now at Google.

168 *"Focus on creating something bigger":* Tom first wrote about Ron Volpe in *The Ten Faces of Innovation* (pp. 117–18). He checked details of the story with Ron by e-mail in March 2011.

168 *One corporate manager we know:* Monica Jerez, interview by Corina Yen and Tom, May 2012. Tom taught a morning session of the "Developing Growth Leaders" class, where he met Monica for a second time.

170 *Didn't see eye to eye:* Lauren Weinstein, interview by Corina Yen, September 2011.

172 *Veteran fifth-grade teacher:* Marcy Barton, interview by Corina Yen, August 2011. Some of the language from this story appeared in a piece by David on Steelcase's "100 Minds" website, http://100.steelcase.com/mind/david-kelley/#page-content-minds.

CHAPTER 6

175 *Cultural transition at Intuit:* We first heard this story in a talk given by Kaaren Hanson at the MX 2011 conference, San Francisco, CA, "Intuit's Reinvention from the Inside," March 2011, http://archive.mxconference .com/2011/videos/kaaren-hanson-video. Further details come from a conversation David and Tom had with Kaaren Hanson and Suzanne Pellican of Intuit in May 2012 (Suzanne now leads the catalysts).

177 *Team observed dozens of young people:* Erica Naone, "Intuit's Big Refresh," *Technology Review Business Report,* April 14, 2011, 26–27.

178 *Company's performance:* Roger L. Martin, "The Innovation Catalysts," *Harvard Business Review,* June 2011, 82–87.

179 *Phases that corporations go through:* Mauro Porcini, interview by Corina Yen and Tom Kelley, November 2011.

181 *"Show, don't tell":* Claudia Kotchka, interview by Corina Yen and Tom Kelley, November 2011.

182 *"Ground troops and air coverage":* Jeremy Utley, interview by Corina Yen and David Kelley, August 2011.

184 *Low on Post-it notes:* IDEO designer Jonah Houston told this story to Corina Yen and Tom in February 2013.

185 *Four thousand unique Post-it products:* See the Post-it website, http:// www.post-it.com/wps/portal/3M/en_US/Post_It/Global/About.

187 *JetBlue:* Bonny Simi, remarks to an Executive Education Bootcamp class at the d.school, March 2011, http://vimeo.com/23341617. For more details and the recovery statistics see Dan Heath and Chip Heath, "Team Coordination Is Key in Businesses," *Fast Company,* July/August 2010, http://www .fastcompany.com/1659112/team-coordination-key-businesses; and Robert Sutton, "A Great Boss is Confident, But Not Really Sure," *HBR Blog Network,* July 15, 2010, http://blogs.hbr.org/sutton/2010/07/a_great_boss _is_confident_but.html.

188 *Estimated $30 million:* This was then CEO David Neeleman's estimate at the end of the crisis, as reported by Grace Wong in "JetBlue fiasco: $30M price tag," *CNNMoney.com,* February 20, 2007, http://money.cnn .com/2007/02/20/news/companies/jet_blue.

189 *OpenIDEO:* OpenIDEO was founded by London-based IDEO designers Tom Hulme, Nathan Waterhouse, and Haiyan Zhang. For more information, go to http://www.openideo.com/. Number of users is as reported on the website (and growing every day), and number of countries is based on Google Analytics data.

*

NOTES

190 **Care and Feeding of an Innovation Team:** Thanks to d.schoolers Peter Rubin and Julian Gorodsky for their help with this list, which is based on the "Ten Principles of Great Teams" that Julian and Peter have used with teams at the d.school.

192 **"Set Designer":** See *The Ten Faces of Innovation* (pp. 194–214). For more about "building your greenhouse" also see *The Art of Innovation* (pp. 121–46).

192 **Classic American brand:** Joerg Student, interview by Corina Yen and Tom Kelley, May 2012.

196 **Make Space:** Scott Doorley and Scott Witthoft, *Make Space: How to Set the Stage for Creative Collaboration* (Hoboken, NJ: Wiley, 2011). The authors have chronicled the d.school space story along with insights and techniques gained along the way. The book has many practical tips—from how to build a z-rack for rolling whiteboards to where to buy versatile stacking foam cubes.

198 **Power of a positive vocabulary:** Tom's kids went through Jim Wiltens's programs in school, and then Tom learned about his material firsthand in a special six-week parent-child evening program. You can learn more about Jim's programs at his website, http://www.jimwiltens.com.

199 **Negative speech patterns:** Cathie Black, *Basic Black: The Essential Guide for Getting Ahead at Work (and in Life)* (New York: Crown Business, 2007), 63.

199 **"How might we":** If you are curious about the history of the "How might we . . ." phrase, check out Warren Berger, "The Secret Phrase Top Innovators Use," *HBR Blog Network*, September 17, 2012, http://blogs.hbr.org/cs/2012/09/the_secret_phrase_top_innovato.html.

201 **"Multipliers":** Liz Wiseman and Greg McKeown, "Bringing Out the Best in Your People," *Harvard Business Review*, May 2010, 117–21. The list for "How to Multiply the Impact of Your Team" is based on the five types of multipliers described in the article. We also recommend Liz Wiseman and Greg McKeown, *Multipliers: How the Best Leaders Make Everyone Smarter* (New York: Harper Collins, 2010).

202 **Study of groups:** Warren Bennis and Patricia Ward Biederman, *Organizing Genius: The Secrets of Creative Collaboration* (New York: Basic Books, 1998). The description of great groups is on pages 201–15. Some of our material about Warren Bennis comes from an all-day session for sixteen storytellers hosted by chairman and CEO of Mandalay Entertainment Group Peter Guber. (Tom was lucky enough to be seated beside Warren for the event.)

•

NOTES

203 *How Procter & Gamble transformed:* Claudia Kotchka, interview by Corina Yen and Tom Kelley, November 2011.

203 *"Cultural alchemist":* "Claudia Kotchka: The Mash-Up Artist," *Businessweek,* June 18, 2006, http://www.businessweek.com/stories/2006-06-18/claudia-kotchka-the-mash-up-artist.

204 *"Transform the company":* Jennifer Reingold, "The Interpreter," *Fast Company,* June 2005, http://www.fastcompany.com/53060/interpreter.

207 *Three hundred facilitators:* Lydia Dishman, "P&G Expands Experience to Make More Innovative Experts," *Fast Company,* February 2013, http://www.fastcompany.com/3004314/pg-expands-experience-make-more-innovative-experts.

207 *"Under Claudia's leadership":* Procter & Gamble, "Procter & Gamble Announces Organizational Changes," press release, May 21, 2008, http://news.pg.com/press-release/pg-corporate-announcements/procter-gamble-announces-organizational-changes-4.

208 *Job washing airplanes:* Sydney Pollack, *Sketches of Frank Gehry,* Sony Pictures Home Entertainment, 2006.

CHAPTER 7

215 *Valuable in all sorts of creative endeavors:* Rolf Faste, *Mind Mapping,* 1997, http://www.fastefoundation.org/publications/mind_mapping.pdf.

218 *"Idea wallets":* Tom talked about idea wallets in *The Ten Faces of Innovation* (p. 18), which he describes as a list that "contains both innovative concepts worth emulating and problems that need solving."

222 *"Empathy map":* For further information about this tool, see the d.school's *Bootcamp Bootleg,* http://dschool.stanford.edu/wp content/uploads/2011/03/BootcampBootleg2010v2SLIM.pdf.

230 *Speed Meeting:* Kara Harrington of IDEO and our colleague Doug Solomon used the special Speed Meeting version of this tool in a session with Nobel laureates in May 2011.

231 *"Nickname Warm-up":* Thanks to Jeremy Utley, Perry Klebahn, and d.school lecturer Kathryn Segovia for their help with this tool and stories of its use, shared with us in an e-mail on January 31, 2013.

237 *The Dream/Gripe Session:* See page 77 of the *Design Thinking for Educators* toolkit, http://designthinkingforeducators.com/toolkit/.

240 *Facilitator's guide:* Get the facilitator's guide for the wallet project from the d.school's website, https://dschool.stanford.edu/groups/designresources/wiki/4dbb2/The_Wallet_Project.html.

245 *"Few people think about":* "Bill Moggridge: 1943–2012," Cooper-Hewitt, National Design Museum website, http://www.cooperhewitt.org/remembering-bill/life-work. Bill lived his whole life with creative confidence and always seemed to warm people around him with his glow.

248 *Bias toward action:* Thanks to Perry Klebahn and Chris Flink for their help thinking about this section in a conversation with David in April 2012.

250 *To start a group of her own:* Stephanie Rowe, interview by Corina Yen and Tom Kelley, October 2011. Some details about Stephanie's Meetup group, Design Thinking DC (DT:DC), come from the group's website, http://designthinkingdc.com.

251 *OpenIDEO:* We encourage everyone to sign up for OpenIDEO as a way to learn more about design thinking, get involved in an empowered community, and start building your creative confidence; go to http://www.openideo.com.

252 *Online resources:* See *Human-Centered Design Toolkit:* http://www.hcdconnect.org, *Design Thinking for Educators* toolkit: http://designthinkingforeducators.com, *Virtual Crash Course:* http://dschool.stanford.edu/dgift, and *Bootcamp Bootleg*: http://dschool.stanford.edu/use-our-methods.

253 *Creatively confident person:* This story is based on an interview conducted by Corina Yen in September 2011.

255 *Nordstrom has an innovation lab:* See Eric Ries, "A Startup Inside a Fortune 500 Company? The Nordstrom Innovation Lab," *Huffington Post*, November 4, 2011, http://www.huffingtonpost.com/eric-ries/a-startup-inside-a-fortun_b_1068449.html.

PHOTO / ILLUSTRATION CREDITS

INTRODUCTION: THE HEART OF INNOVATION

page xvi Chapter illustration ©Alyana Cazalet

1. FLIP: FROM DESIGN THINKING TO CREATIVE CONFIDENCE

page 12 Chapter illustration ©Alyana Cazalet
page 17 Photo courtesy of Children's Hospital of Pittsburgh of UPMC
page 19 Illustration by Beau Bergeron
page 29 Photo courtesy of the d.school

2. DARE: FOM FEAR TO COURAGE

page 36 Chapter illustration ©Alyana Cazalet
page 60 Illustration by Dan Roam
page 61 Illustration by Dan Roam

3. SPARK: FROM BLANK PAGE TO INSIGHT

page 66 Chapter illustration ©Alyana Cazalet
page 70 Photo courtesy of Embrace
page 92 Photo courtesy of IDEO/Nicolas Zurcher

4. LEAP: FROM PLANNING TO ACTION

page 108 Chapter illustration ©Alyana Cazalet
page 113 Photo courtesy of Anirudh Rao
page 133 Photo courtesy of IDEO/Nicolas Zurcher
page 134 Photo courtesy of IDEO/Nicolas Zurcher
page 137 Photo courtesy of Walgreen Co.
page 138 Illustration by Beau Bergeron

5. SEEK: FROM DUTY TO PASSION

6. TEAM: CREATIVELY CONFIDENT GROUPS

7. MOVE: CREATIVE CONFIDENCE TO GO

8. NEXT: EMBRACE CREATIVE CONFIDENCE

INDEX